PR techniques that work

Jim Dunn

HAWKSMERE

Published by Hawksmere plc
12-18 Grosvenor Gardens
London SW1W 0DH.

© Jim Dunn 1999

All rights reserved. No part of this publication may be reproduced, stored in a retrieval system or transmitted in any form or by any means, electronic, photocopying, recording or otherwise, without the prior permission of the publisher.

This Pocketbook is sold subject to the condition that it shall not, by way of trade or otherwise, be lent, re-sold, hired out or otherwise circulated without the publisher's prior consent in any form of binding or cover other than in which it is published and without a similar condition including this condition being imposed upon the subsequent purchaser.

No responsibility for loss occasioned to any person acting or refraining from action as a result of any material in this publication can be accepted by the author or publisher.

A CIP catalogue record for this Pocketbook is available from the British Library.

ISBN 1 85418 187 4

Printed in Great Britain by Ashford Colour Press.

Designed and typeset by Paul Wallis for Hawksmere.

Business Action Pocketbooks

Business Action Pocketbooks are concise but comprehensive reference books designed to fit in your pocket or briefcase to be a ready source of business information.

Pocketbooks will be of use to anyone involved in business. For owner managers and for managers in bigger businesses they will provide an introduction to the topic; for people already familiar with the topic they provide a ready reminder of key requirements. Each section concludes with a checklist of useful tips.

Other titles in the 'Pocketbook' series

Business Action Pocketbooks are a series of concise but comprehensive reference books. Each one contains sections describing particular aspects of a topic in detail and checklists with useful tips.

Building Your Business

This *Pocketbook* provides practical information about growth, strategy and business planning. Effective leadership, problem solving, decision making and the formal aspects of running a business are also covered in this guide which will help to define your strategy and ensure that you achieve your stake in the future.

Managing and Employing People
Discover the key to successful people management by motivating, stimulating and rewarding your staff. Practical information and advice about recruiting staff, employee rights and obligations, effectively managing people and the legal aspects of employment are all covered in this *Pocketbook*.

Finance and Profitability
Practical tips and techniques for profitable management, including costing and budgeting, record keeping and using financial statements and understanding and finding investment are given in this *Pocketbook*. There is also advice on financial forecasting, monitoring performance against your plans and retaining effective financial control. This book will help ensure that your business is successful and profitable.

Sales and Marketing
This *Pocketbook* is an excellent reference tool focusing on the overall process of sales and marketing. It will help give you a direction and a set of goals along with practical tips and techniques for successful market research, segmentation and planning, promoting, selling and exporting. It will help you take those first important steps towards establishing a presence in your market.

Developing Yourself and Your Staff
Team building, personal development, managing meetings, stimulating staff and quality management are all covered in a clear and practical way for the busy manager in this *Pocketbook*. By developing

your people through teamwork, training and empowerment you are developing your business – this book tells you how.

Effective Business Communications
Effective communications are vital to the success of a business. Every business needs to be able to communicate in a number of ways – to customers, staff, owners and other shareholders – in writing, visually and in person. This *Pocketbook* provides an introduction to different forms of communication for a range of purposes. The way a business communicates, and the information it provides, are of paramount importance to the business's ability to survive and prosper.

Managing Projects and Operations
In any business, tasks may be continuous, such as production lines, or stand alone, discrete projects. All need to be carefully managed, with targets and milestones, if you are to maximise efficiency and effectiveness. This *Pocketbook* provides an introduction to task management including decision making, corporate policies, planning and systems.

John Adair on Leadership
This book is a practical master class in how to manage both yourself and others to provide a team that is motivated, creative and high-performing. It covers time management, setting and achieving goals, decision making and problem solving, creativity and innovation, team building, motivation and people management, communication and presentation.

The author

Jim Dunn has had nearly 30 years in public relations. Following six years in journalism in Britain, he started his own public relations company, TPS Public Relations, in 1969 in the heart of the then British media centre, Fleet Street in London.

As a former journalist, he believes strongly that a good public relations practitioner should ideally have a background in newspapers or magazines. 'If this is not the case,' he says, 'anyone coming into public relations should make their first task that of visiting a newspaper, talking to the journalists and finding out how they work and what they require from a public relations person. I'm continually concerned about the lack of understanding of a journalist's job by some public relations people.'

'There is no mystique surrounding good public relations,' he says. 'Good public relations is based on common sense, an alert mind and creativity: of knowing just how much you can accomplish with public relations; accepting that you can't win them all and having the ability to move on to the next exercise when an idea doesn't succeed.'

Contents

Introduction 1

1 The nature of public relations 3

PR: some definitions 3

Scope 4

The key elements 9

The lesson to be learned 10

Useful tips 11

2 The role and function of a PRO 13

The case for a consultancy 15

Engaging a PR consultancy
– the top ten tips 16

The case for in-house PR 17

Combining in-house PR
and consultancy 18

What makes a successful PRO? 19

The PRO's job brief 21

Useful tips 22

3 Costing PR **25**

　　Establishing the parameters 26

　　The distinct cost elements 27

　　Getting value for money 28

　　Useful tips 29

4 How to deal with the media – Dunn's golden rules **31**

　　Media 'manners' 31

　　What is the story for the media? 34

　　What is *not* a story? 37

　　Useful tips 39

5 Setting up and operating the PR office **41**

　　Photographic library 41

　　Biographies and how to write them 42

　　Background releases
　　– the middle ground 46

　　Press releases and how
　　to write them 50

　　The good and the bad 55

　　Useful tips 60

6 Preparing feature articles 63
Feature articles: Case history 65
Useful tips 71

7 Public relations photography 73
Finding a photographer 73
Photo opportunities 74
How to present the photograph 79
Useful tips 80

8 Press conferences, media events and interviews 83
Press conferences 83
Media events 87
Face-to-face interviews 88
Press lunches 89
Media visits 91
Useful tips 94

9 Be effective on radio or television 97
Media interview techniques 98
Checklist: effective interviews 101
Interview training 105
Useful tips 106

10 PR on a small budget 109
The hotel scenario 110
Useful tips 114

11 New product launches 115
Launch theme and date 115
Venue 116
Refreshments 116
Guest list and invitations 116
Photography 117
Client briefing 117
Press kits 117
Special media requirements 117
Useful tips 118

12 Crisis public relations: How to handle emergencies 121
The guidelines 121
Crisis PR in practice 124
Taking disaster management seriously: An example 127
Conclusion 137
Useful tips 137

Introduction

This book is intended to help you, and your company, get the best out of the media through effective public relations. It sets out to ask, and answer, questions facing everyone involved in PR at whatever level, from chief executives, marketing directors and sales managers to newly appointed public relations officers (PROs) or those who have been in the profession for some time but realise there is still a lot to learn.

- What is PR?
- How can it be used to promote my company, organisation or product?
- Can I make use of PR even with a small budget?
- How do I write an effective press release?
- Do syndicated features work?
- What is 'news' and what isn't?
- How should I deal with the media?
- How do I cope in the event of a disaster or emergency?

These are just some of the many themes tackled in this book, which covers the gamut of PR activities and skills which now, more than ever, are being used by large and small companies, national and multi-national corporations, organisations of all types and sizes, and even political parties, to get their message across.

1 The nature of public relations

Confusion about what public relations is and what it can, and cannot, achieve is still rife, so here is a selection of definitions, each emphasising slightly different aspects of the activity.

PR: some definitions

- The projection of the personality of a company or organisation

- The organised two-way communications between an organisation and the audiences critical to its success, the aim being to create understanding and support for its objectives, policies and actions

- The management activity responsible for the creation of favourable attitudes among key audiences

- An 'exercise in diplomacy': putting the facts and viewpoints of the client to whatever 'jury' is appropriate – government, the buying public, shareholders, a committee of inquiry, Members of Parliament or whatever

- Something that embraces all the activities that build good relations with audiences, attempting to change negative or incorrect opinions and reinforce positive or correct ones. In other words, projecting a 'good feeling' for an organisation and turning the negative into the positive.

Scope

The 'official' definition of PR, from the Institute of Public Relations, is: 'the planned and sustained effort to establish and maintain goodwill and mutual understanding between an organisation and its publics'.

PR has many elements, publicity being one of the most important. This seeks to inform readers, listeners or viewers, and to be effective must have news value, something the media and PR professionals call a 'news angle'. A story must hang on a peg to be carried by the media; if it is of little or no interest to the audience it will not interest the reporter or editor, even if he or she is someone you have deliberately courted over the years.

Another element of PR is promotion, which also aims to inform, although existing mainly to project the benefits of a programme or product, and is more akin to advertising than publicity; this is why promotional articles are more difficult to place in the news media, since they usually lack a strong 'news angle'.

Although public relations is at last becoming appreciated as an important factor in the success of any organisation, some companies still engage in protracted discussions on whether they should 'have' PR or not. This is ridiculous, since all organisations are communicating with audiences that are important to them – in other words practising PR – whether they realise it or not.

The decision, therefore, is not whether to 'have' PR but whether these PR activities should be handled in a planned, organised manner or allowed to be haphazard, possibly inconsistent, and almost certainly ineffective and inefficient.

Increasingly, public relations is seen as an essential top management responsibility not an optional extra or an add-on publicity gimmick, with companies and organisations now giving the development of a worthwhile PR policy as much thought, attention and professional skill as their financial or personnel policies.

Good PR certainly needs thought, planning and organisation. Indeed, while it should always be a welcoming host to bright ideas, it demands, if it is to be both effective and economical, as vigilant and exacting a programme of planning, preparation, timing and execution as any other job. Business, however efficient, must continuously study its PR needs and opportunities since it must not only *be* efficient but must be *seen* to be efficient.

However, PR is only ever as good as the product. The best PR will not compensate for weakness in business areas, and companies need to attract the right personnel and train, develop and motivate them.

The PR industry is making major efforts to train professional people to take on the most senior levels of responsibility, and the new generation of highly educated entrants to the profession expect to share corporate responsibility in the boardroom, alongside the established professionals such as engineers, accountants and solicitors.

Good PR people understandably want to prove their value by their creativity, their contribution to improved efficiency, greater commercial success, industrial expansion and better human relations.

PR officers or consultants can play a key role in building up goodwill, providing that their activities are within the framework of an agreed and understood corporate policy. The PR professional can help management to agree on the 'personality' that the company, corporation or organisation wishes to develop and project, and the practical PR actions that will achieve this.

Important groups of people, for example, tend to be overlooked when all is going smoothly, but when the going gets tough their goodwill may be essential. However, this is also the least appropriate time to appeal to them. Employees who receive proper communications when industrial harmony reigns may be more sympathetic when potential disputes arise.

In a nutshell; good public relations should embrace the professional strategy of planning in advance of what opinion the public will hold concerning your product or organisation, because a carefully planned, comprehensive public relations campaign is the most effective and economical means of creating in the public mind a favourable impression or a desire for a product.

There is a tendency in Great Britain (although attitudes are changing), as opposed to the US where PR has been much more fully developed, to compare and confuse public relations with advertising. In fact, they are quite separate and distinct, and their impact on the general public is entirely different.

Advertising occupies space which the reader knows has been bought. No matter how attractively advertising material is presented, no matter how factual it is, it is bound to meet with some reservations: the manufacturer, whom not even the most generous and open-minded reader would consider impartial, has obviously got an interest at stake.

The art of public relations is to have the appearance of disinterestedness. It stands to reason that the facts regarding the merits of any company or product are more readily believed if they are put forward with apparent spontaneity by a person or body not directly concerned with increasing its sales.

It must be conceded that the image of the PR industry, until recently, was not good at all. People were very wary about PR companies and PR executives, and often quite justifiably. But, thankfully, the image of the PR man in the 1960s strutting down Fleet Street in pin-stripes and carnation to buy a bottle or two of Muscadet at El Vino's at lunchtime is now almost dead, not just because the 'action' has transferred from Fleet Street to Wapping and elsewhere, but because the PR profession has 'grown up' and journalists have grown up alongside it. The recession of the late 1980s and early 1990s has also put paid to the long lunch!

Today's journalists are much more willing to listen to the views of the PR executive than their predecessors, and most would admit that they would find their jobs more difficult were it not for the help and advice of professional PROs.

While the overall attitude towards PR is now much more favourable than before, several things irritate those in the industry about the way it is perceived, even by those with considerable experience of it. One such irritation is that PR is often seen as a luxury, to be indulged in only in times of prosperity, or, conversely, in times of emergency. In fact, it is especially important during a trade recession, ensuring that the public understands both the reasons for the policies being pursued and the difficulties that the enterprise is facing, and contributing directly to the removal of these difficulties.

The key elements

Put simply, then, public relations is all about communications, an over-used word but one whose importance should not be overlooked. And there are three key elements to the communications process, as follows.

What do you want to say?

The message is crucial. There is no point in using PR techniques for the sake of it. Your message may be to inform customers about a new product, or shareholders about planned activities; to tell employees about a factory closure or suppliers about a change in distribution patterns. Before putting pen to paper, or calling on the services of the PRO, establish what message, what 'angle' you want to try to put across. Bear in mind that it should be 'newsy' or controversial to stand a reasonable chance of making any impression or being taken up by the media.

Who are you trying to reach?

Clearly this must depend on the message you are trying to put across. But don't forget that there are many distinct and separate target groups that you should seek to influence. There are obvious ones such as your customers, but even this target group needs to be broken down into smaller targets: housewives on estates, to take one extreme, or customers for left-handed screwdrivers, to take another.

Then there are the not-so-obvious groups such as civil servants, MPs or local authorities, all of whom can make a major impact on your business.

Increasingly important is informing the financial community of what is happening. Good investor relations can help keep your share price up and be of crucial importance during takeover bids, either when you are on the defensive or the attack.

How can you get your message across?
This is where good PR comes into its own. PROs who are professional know which medium to aim for: trade or national press, or radio and television. They can also suggest when it will be more effective to use sponsorship, exhibitions, direct mail, or a combination of several, to do the job.

The lesson to be learned

A spokesman for a major brewing company commented on his company's public awareness: 'Our brands are well known and that's what counts. We don't care if nobody knows the name of our company.'

Successive generations of financial journalists found out that the company meant just that; it was one of the most difficult companies to contact. Subsequently the company became very much in need of friends in the financial press when it found itself on the wrong end of a takeover bid from a major rival. In the end the price of saving itself from its rival's clutches was to be taken over by another company; one which had assiduously wooed, by all accounts, the financial press and institutions.

Effective PR will ensure that the public that is important to you is no longer ignorant of your good points, of your special strengths, your achievements and the difficulties that you are meeting and have overcome. The result of this increased knowledge will be greater understanding of your problems, greater appreciation of your achievements, greater interest in your business and quicker recognition of your products.

USEFUL TIPS

- *Public relations is the planned and sustained effort to establish and maintain goodwill and mutual understanding between an organisation and its publics (Institute of Public Relations).*

- *Publicity is one of the most important elements of PR, along with promotion.*

- *Good public relations should embrace the professional strategy of planning in advance of what opinion the public will hold concerning your product or organisation.*

> *A carefully planned, comprehensive public relations campaign is the most effective and economical means of creating in the public mind a favourable impression or a desire for a product.*

2 The role and function of a PRO

Once a company or organisation has decided to examine and tackle its public relations needs and objectives, there are a number of options available.

The three main ones are:

- The appointment of an outside consultancy
- The nomination and training of an existing executive to handle the public relations responsibilities
- The appointment of professional PR staff.

Sometimes the ideal solution may be a combination of more than one of these three methods.

One of the major factors in deciding which route to pursue will be the company's level of commitment to good PR. If it is operating in a competitive market, under public scrutiny, and possibly in a sensitive area, it will find PR absolutely fundamental to trading success, and will require skilled executives, whether staff or consultancy or a mixture of both.

Some organisations, such as companies with near-monopoly situations, statutory bodies, professional associations and some government authorities, may feel that they can relegate PR to a lower level of importance. Others have an equally narrow view of the role of public relations, giving their executives such limiting titles as press officer or, even more restricting, information officer. Clearly a press officer is responsible for only part of a broad PR function. Press relations, however effectively operated, are only a part of public relations.

Many organisations have to rely on voluntary or untrained assistance in PR because of the limits on their budgets. This is often the case with voluntary groups, churches, small charities, local arts societies and the like. But even with a very small or non-existent budget, PR techniques can still be employed to excellent effect, especially if there is a PR professional within the society or community who has an interest in the particular cause and can be persuaded to lend his or her expertise in a voluntary capacity. (See Chapter 10.)

Frequently the reason a PR budget is not available is simply that the company does not rate the importance of the PR function highly enough. If the management can argue that it does not need a significant PR resource, this may be an acceptable point for debate, but to contend that it cannot afford a proper resource is very questionable.

Effective PR ultimately costs no more than poor PR. The returns from an investment in public relations are usually so significant that a company has to be spending a very substantial amount of money before it reaches a point of diminishing returns.

The case for a consultancy

The appointment of a professional public relations consultant can result in maximum impact. The size and diversity of the media is the overwhelming argument in favour of employing an outside consultant, for only a group specialising in PR can supply experts in the many different fields of publicity available today.

For a company to try to set up, within its own organisation, a department to cope successfully with all the outlets available to it can necessitate the employment of several senior executives, each expert in a particular field. The cost of this, together with secretarial assistance and office equipment, can be prohibitive for all but the largest firms.

Another handicap a company or organisation faces in trying to undertake its own public relations is that it is often too close to its own subject. The temptation to preach to people who are already on your side is difficult to resist.

An outside consultant, on the other hand, can take a detached view of your business and maintain a viewpoint of impartiality, and is in a much better position to present your case to the vital segments of the public you wish to reach.

Engaging a PR consultancy – the top ten tips

If you are planning to employ a consultancy, here are some guidelines:

1. Don't let yourself be hoodwinked by wonderful, flashy, tap-dancing presentations
2. Don't be intimidated by great theorising on 'market segmentations'
3. Question those bidding for your PR business closely on what direct media experience they have
4. Question who they know in the media
5. Question what success they have had in the PR field in the past
6. Ask to meet the account director(s) who will work with you
7. Talk to the media yourself for recommendations of consultancies you should see. Your trade media will be a good barometer in this area
8. See no more than three consultancies. If you can't make up your mind after seeing three, you never will
9. Suck it and see… working with any consultancy in the early stages is always an experiment. Insist on an early review of the contract
10. Be wary of big international agencies except those with smaller regional offices. PR is a very personal business and you could get lost in a large organisation.

The case for in-house PR

Appointing an in-house PRO is becoming commonplace among large companies and organisations aware of the need to communicate effectively and creatively with the public and their own workforce. The advantages of doing so are obvious, not least the fact that the PRO is on hand most of the time to respond immediately to management's requests or briefings, and by being involved day-to-day in the company's operations can be totally familiar with all the developments taking place and all the areas lending themselves to promotion.

A skilled in-house PRO, therefore, can contribute a great deal to the way a company is perceived by the media and the public, especially if allowed to become actively involved at the policy-making stage when decisions are taken that affect the company's image and character.

Unfortunately, however, in a misguided attempt to contain costs, too many companies give the post of internal PRO to bright secretaries who, while almost certainly having the right personalities and right attitudes for the job, lack even the most basic of the necessary skills. As I hope this book demonstrates, the myths and mystiques surrounding public relations are largely imaginary but for it to be successful, PR does require a great many skills and talents on the part of the practitioner, not least a thorough understanding of the media, something a promoted secretary won't have.

Combining in-house PR and consultancy

An ever-increasing number of companies and organisations are tackling their PR requirements these days on two fronts: by establishing an in-house PR department and, at the same time, engaging the services of a specialist outside consultancy.

The advantages of this dual approach to PR are obvious. Not only does it give the company or organisation peace of mind knowing that there is a PR practitioner just down the corridor who can be totally involved and immersed in the company, its plans and its developments, but in knowing, too, that it has the added advantage of a pool of professional PR expertise to call upon to formulate and carry out skilled PR activities.

Engaging the services of a PR consultancy alone, without the back-up of an in-house PR department, can have its drawbacks, since account directors at most PR consultancies handle several clients at any one time, and there can be occasions when their priorities differ from those of the company paying the fee.

But even the 'combination' approach to PR can come unstuck unless channels of communication and accountability are clearly established and monitored. The need for the correct internal set-up to feed the agency with good quality material to enable it to use its professionalism to best effect is vital. It is not appreciated how critical it is to establish the internal set-up correctly in order to get the most out of a PR consultancy relationship.

Of particular importance in this respect is the establishment of a central point of contact to deal with the consultancy and the myriad enquiries and queries that emerge. Unless the internal PRO is of sufficient standing and experience, this function should be allocated to a senior executive such as the marketing director.

Despite the possible pitfalls, however, a combination of in-house and consultancy PR does make good sense, and can be a very powerful tool if the set-up is right.

What makes a successful PRO?

Whether you opt for an in-house PRO, a consultancy, or a combination of the two, having the right person working on your behalf is obviously of prime importance. To help you in the selection process, here is a list of qualities, attributes and skills which, from experience, I believe are important in a good PRO:

- An ex-journalist or media person who has had some working knowledge of the media, and who knows and recognises its needs, as well as the tricks of the trade
- Someone who has an uncomplicated approach
- A person with a neat and tidy mind – a lot of PR is tying up loose ends, and administration
- Someone who gets on well with people
- Someone who doesn't mind being at the beck and call of the media for 24 hours a day –

the communications industry doesn't work from 9-5

- Someone for whom nothing is too much trouble
- Someone who can string several paragraphs together in their proper order to form an interesting story – lack of this ability is the major complaint from the media
- Someone who doesn't think he/she is God's gift to the media
- Someone with patience and common sense.

On the whole, the best PROs are, as I indicated, broadcasters or journalists who have been able to make that very difficult switch over the fence. They know how the system works on the other side, and that is a great help.

If, on the other hand, a new PR entrant's route has been via a university or college course, he or she should get into a radio or television station and a newspaper office – even for a day – to see how the system works at grass roots; see how a programme is put together; see how the columnist selects his/her topics.

There's a lot of new technology in PR, but technology won't help PR practitioners unless they understand the basics… what constitutes a story; how to interest the target media in it; and how to present the facts. Whatever path you take, the functions of the PR professional remain basically the same.

Beware the rip-off merchants

The bad image acquired by PR and the PR industry in the past in the UK is partly the fault of the practitioners themselves, both in-house and in consultancies. That is why it has taken British industry a long time to realise the considerable benefits to be gained from positive and professional PR advice.

Of course, there are still rip-off merchants in our industry. There will always be people who will grab the retainer fee, blind you with science, but fail to deliver the promised media coverage.

But the industry is gradually sifting out the wheat from the chaff.

The PRO's job brief

- To establish a PR information library; get together the important company news; and be ready and prepared when the media calls

- To initiate media coverage of organisation or company activities, people, services and products through targeted media

- To act as spokesperson for the organisation with no other member of staff being authorised to answer questions from the media, unless under clearly defined circumstances or as part of a planned media-briefing session; and to keep the number of people authorised to speak to the media as small as possible

- To write and issue press releases to the relevant targeted media, whether trade, local, national or whatever, with approval of senior management being obtained before any release is issued

- To keep in touch with media contacts
- To plan an organisation's PR effort strategically
- To be creatively tactical in the PR effort to, say, sell or move sluggish products.

USEFUL TIPS

> *The appointment of a professional public relations consultant can result in maximum impact. Before a consultant is appointed question their previous track record and who they know in the media. Don't be intimidated and don't be hoodwinked by a flashy presentation.*

> *An in-house PRO can also contribute a great deal to the way a company is perceived by the media and the public, especially if they are allowed to become actively involved in policy making.*

> *An increasing number of companies employ a consultant and an in-house PRO to maximise their PR operation. One central point of contact, however, must be established.*

> *On the whole, the best PROs are broadcasters and journalists who know how the system works – on both sides of the fence.*

> *The PRO should be ready and prepared when the media calls, should keep in touch with the media, initiate media coverage and be able to plan an organisation's PR effort strategically.*

3 Costing PR

Historically the public relations elements of the overall marketing budget has tended to be the 'poor relations' afterthought. In recent years, however, this entrenched attitude has been gradually changing as a more realistic understanding of the cost-effective nature of PR has emerged.

In considering the relative merits of developing an in-house PR facility, as opposed to the use of outside consultancies, cost is frequently cited as a major influencing factor. This argument has been used as a justification in favour of both approaches over the years.

In truth, of course, this decision should be based on careful consideration as to how a company's image development and projection can be best served.

The smoke screen of cost is a common phenomenon and one which is frequently used in cases of major disappointment and sometimes serious problems when much-vaunted PR campaigns fail. Such failures can arise equally from over-generous as from parsimonious budgets. Lack of resources or over-lavish expenditure can, of course, be a factor in failure but the root cause will be elsewhere: in poor planning, execution or allocation of whatever budget *is* available.

Establishing the parameters

Any sensible comment on the cost of PR must be prefaced by establishing certain parameters.

First, it must be assumed that PR is to be approached from a professional viewpoint. I have known many organisations – some very large – whose entire PR capability is staffed by junior personnel 'promoted' from other functions for a variety of nebulous reasons. This is not only a mockery of the whole concept of effective media and public relations, but serves to distort the perception of acceptable budget levels both at the outset and on a continuing basis as the results achieved fail to match up to expectations.

Second, if an in-house facility is to be established as opposed to use of a consultancy on the basis of cost, it is important to consider in the relative calculations all those ancillary costs so often ignored in such an exercise.

Remember that fees paid to a consultancy will cover not only salaries but all staff costs such as NI, pension, benefits, holiday pay, sickness and holiday cover. Also included are office accommodation, secretarial back-up, management and training.

Finally, if a consultancy is the preferred approach, it must be assumed that a professional selection appraisal has taken place and that the common pitfalls of performance-related contracts, executive time restricted agreements and offers of patently non-commercial fee levels have been avoided.

The distinct cost elements

Public relations, as with most marketing disciplines, will have two distinct cost elements – fixed costs (salary and establishment costs of the in-house department or fees to the consultancy) and directly related operating expenses (telephones, travel, entertaining, photography, printing, etc). The level of operating expenses is unlikely to vary significantly between a consultancy and an in-house department – they are those unavoidable necessities of operating an effective campaign.

In the author's experience there is a remarkably consistent relationship between the level of operating expenses and the fixed costs. For many years we have advised allowing an expense budget at a level of 30 per cent of fixed costs. As to salaries and fees, there are no rules of thumb as to what proportion of marketing budget should be allocated in this direction. So much depends on the size of the company, its objectives, the value placed on PR, the industry and the disciplines included under the general PR budget head.

It is true certainly that salary levels in the PR field have increased considerably over the past few years as the understanding of the profession has developed. This boom has resulted in a shortage of talented and experienced professionals who have been able to command even higher remuneration.

This position is further aggravated by a serious lack of proper training facilities for promising recruits. So much of the skills of PR can only develop effectively in an operating environment, working with a group of experienced personnel. Such conditions are unusual in anything but the really large commercial concerns, and most training and on-the-job experience therefore derives from consultancies.

Having invested much time and money in training promising newcomers, consultancies will fight hard to retain the best, adding further to the salary spiral.

There are some signs that the substantial influx of new talent over recent years has now provided the PR business with a satisfactory pool of labour and that there is now a more enlightened attitude to recruitment and training. This should result in more sensible salary conditions and avoid a repetition of the recent salary explosion.

Getting value for money

What is now clear is that the cost of good PR personnel is equivalent to that of qualified accountants, solicitors, doctors and most other professionals.

In this environment, consultancies – faced with ever-increasing costs – have had to adapt rapidly in order to remain competitive. This is not unusual in today's climate but PR is, and will remain, a very labour-intensive industry. Personal contact – its most important tool – cannot be replaced by word processors and computers. None the less, a much more structured approach is now generally taken, with teams working on a range of accounts in order to make best use of scarce and valuable resources.

So, always remember that you get what you pay for in PR. There are no bargains. Many of the London consultancies with international links will tell you that their minimum fee currently is in the region of £35,000 plus expenses, while a medium-sized consultancy perhaps specialising in a particular industry will have a minimum retainer fee of about £20,000. You will probably meet a PR company that will be prepared to work for less than this. *But beware*: it will probably not have the expertise and will certainly restrict the amount of time spent on your work.

The best way, of course, is to decide on your PR budget, tell your consultancy and demand to know what you get in return for this. And then make sure that you have an internal system set up to keep track of your consultancy and see that you do get what you pay for.

USEFUL TIPS

> *Public relations will have two distinct cost elements – fixed costs (salary and establishment costs of the in-house department or fees to the consultancy) and directly related operating expenses (telephones, travel, entertaining, printing etc).*

> *The level of operating expenses is unlikely to vary significantly between a consultancy and an in-house department.*

> *Decide on your PR budget, tell your consultancy and demand to know what you get in return for this.*

> *Set up an internal system to keep track of your consultancy and see that you get what you pay for.*

4 How to deal with the media – Dunn's golden rules

Dealing with the media in all its forms is one of the most important and most difficult aspects of a PRO's role, and it is vital that it is handled professionally and competently.

Many people, including top executives, are wary of journalists, sometimes with good reason. Perhaps they have had bad experiences with reporters in the past, resulting in unfavourable or damaging publicity, or perhaps they simply instinctively distrust them. Whatever the reasons, there is no doubt that a great many people are reluctant to meet journalists, are cagey about giving interviews, and are generally suspicious of the breed, if not actually fearful.

Media 'manners'

This is where a good PR officer can help, because he or she will be accustomed to press and radio/TV reporters. They will be – or should be – on first name terms with many of them, and will know what reporters are like, how they should be handled to achieve the best results. Whether they should be invited for an elaborate lunch, or simply a glass of wine; whether a particular reporter accepts group media visits (many journalists don't, preferring to travel alone); and a hundred-and-one other things that can make the difference between a face-to-face interview or media visit being a success and therefore resulting in favourable editorial coverage or otherwise.

Although effective dealing with the media is a skilled task, there are several rules that should be applied by anyone asked to give an interview to a journalist or simply in their day-to-day dealings:

- If a journalist telephones with an enquiry about your company/organisation or its facilities, ensure that the call is returned as soon as possible. The media works to tight deadlines, and failure to respond quickly can result in missed opportunities for media exposure

- When a journalist is offered facilities, make sure that all the relevant departments/personnel are informed in advance of the visit as far down the line as possible

- The author recommends *never* telling the media anything 'off the record'. If you don't want them to know something, don't tell them. Many PROs disagree with this advice, so how you tackle this thorny problem is, therefore, a personal decision. Bear in mind, however, that it is the media's job to get a story, and although you may give your 'confidential' information to only one journalist on the understanding that what you say won't be printed or broadcast, you never know to whom that journalist may subsequently talk, or what information may be passed on to some less scrupulous fellow journalist

- When inviting media representatives for meetings, the PRO should do the necessary 'homework' in advance so everyone is fully briefed on the nature of the publication or radio/television programme, and is aware of what angles the journalist is likely to pursue

- Make sure you have a comprehensive library of good, clear, black-and-white and colour, photographs of your 'product' and of yourself and senior department heads. Although colour photographs are more attractive and are being increasingly used in glossy magazines, the majority of newspapers and magazines still use black-and-white illustrations exclusively, for reasons of cost, time and technology

- Don't keep chasing up journalists who have interviewed you or department heads to find out when the article will be published. It places them in an awkward position, and is usually a decision not in the writers' control but in that of their features editors, news editors or editors. By 'checking up' afterwards you are only likely to cause, at worst, intimidation, or, at best, embarrassment

- Don't over-indulge journalists with food or drink in the hope that you can 'buy' good editorial. By all means be hospitable, but don't overdo it

- Don't show journalists audio-visuals or videos unless they are professionally produced. Poorly made ones can destroy a carefully built reputation

- Be very selective about the photos/releases you issue to the media. The fact that a 'famous' personality has visited your establishment or bought or sampled your product is no guarantee that the media is likely to be interested in publicising the fact

- Don't issue photos of people lined up in front of the camera holding drinks. Instead, try to be creative about photo make-up. (See section 7.)

- Don't just mail out press releases to all and sundry and hope for the best. Consider the content of the releases and be realistic about those publications that are likely to use them. This implies close familiarity with the media and the type of stories and photographs they carry. The construction and use of press releases is considered below.

What is the story for the media?

So, what is a story for the media – or what happens when Joan Collins isn't news?

It used to be said that 'Dog Bites Man isn't a story, but that Man Bites Dog is'. This, of course, is a gross over-simplification of what is a complex question, but does highlight one of the most important elements in determining what constitutes 'news' and what doesn't – namely interest value. A 'news' story must be of interest; if it isn't, it won't grab the attention of the reporter or news editor.

Another important element is immediacy. An event that happened a week ago is not 'news' except possibly for weekly newspapers or periodicals. Study the national newspapers and you'll understand my point. Virtually all the news items, as opposed to the feature articles, will have an immediacy value: events or developments which happened the previous day or, better still, in the early hours of the morning. As far as national newspapers and radio/television stations are concerned, old news simply isn't news at all, and won't be published or broadcast.

Of course, what constitutes important 'news' to one newspaper won't necessarily be of such importance to its competitors. *The Sun* or the *Daily Mirror*, for example is quite likely to give page 1 splash prominence to Joan Collins or Elizabeth Taylor and their latest boyfriends/husbands, whereas the same information will perhaps receive scant attention in the columns of *The Times* or *The Daily Telegraph*, if it is carried at all, that is.

Why? Because 'news' has to be not only immediate but also of interest to the readers/listeners/viewers and the activities of Collins or Taylor may well be considered of paramount interest to *Sun* or *Daily Mirror* readers, but of little concern or relevance to those who read *The Times*.

So, what constitutes news largely depends on the media you are tackling. Is it local media, national media or your trade press? Is it the 'quality' press or 'popular' press? These are important considerations and you must be clear in your mind what audience you wish to interest, and whether your proposed 'news' items, no matter how immediate and up-to-the-minute, will do the trick.

That said, the following story ideas would appeal to a greater or lesser extent to most sectors of the media:

- Major developments within your company or organisation

- Revolutionary new products

- Spectacular sales figures

- Takeover bids or financial news

- Research on your particular market or industry. You only have to look at the massive coverage that the building societies, for example, obtain when they issue house price surveys around the country, to realise this

- Controversial statements by you on your industry. Always remember that journalists have newspapers/magazines to fill, and they have to fill them with interesting and lively 'copy'. The more lively you can make your comments or observations within the bounds of the politics of your industry, the better

- Expansion schemes such as new headquarters or factories. And, of course, these days – job creation!

What is *not* a story?

Once again, what is not a story depends on the journalist you are speaking to, and the publication or TV/radio station involved, but as a rule:

- Getting a celebrity to launch a new product at a vast fee does not always ensure media coverage except perhaps at a local level. The celebrity, especially a minor one, is not necessarily a story unless he/she has some particular and relevant connection or association with the product. You have to ensure that you build on the celebrity's appearance and the product, and 'create' a news story

  Often, hiring a top celebrity can produce excellent coverage for the celebrity, but nothing at all for your company or product. Photographers may turn out in their droves to snap an 'EastEnders' or 'Coronation Street' star opening a new supermarket, but the chances are that, while the pictures of him or her may receive prominent coverage, nothing – or, at best, very little – is likely to appear in print about the supermarket, defeating the whole object of the exercise

  Treat celebrities for what they are: crowd pullers. They'll get the 'punters' along, but you should build onto that appearance a good, positive media story – job creation or local environmental improvement, for example

  Remember that celebrities are ten-a-penny in the media world, and hiring one for that important opening or product launch could prove a costly mistake

- Marginal increases in sales or performance targets are of little interest. Your figures have to show a spectacular increase, and if they don't it is perhaps best to talk about your industry's performance in general in a particular year, providing this can be shown to be spectacular or impressive, and weave into it details of your own figures and performance

- A facility visit to a factory or new headquarters is seldom sufficient to provide good media coverage. Instead, you need to build on the visit by introducing new angles such as increased job creation or new equipment.

It is important to remember, too, that a company may sometimes be thrust suddenly into the spotlight of public interest when it does not expect to be, and on an issue that it has not anticipated. If its actions at that time are not presented skillfully – if in fact, it is not already practising effective public relations – an unfavourable impression can be fixed so firmly in the general public's mind that it becomes difficult to shift.

Careful targeting of the media is required in the PR business. Blanket mailing of press releases is not effective PR.

At the same time it is not sufficient merely to have an interesting story to tell. That story must be 'sold' to the media – whether it be a newspaper, an illustrated magazine, a film, a technical journal or a radio programme – through which it will make the maximum impact on the desired audience.

If you do decide on a media release, keep it short and simple with no adjectives and no waffle. But don't always resort to a release: most of them are thrown away, certainly by the cynical news editors of the national media. Instead, a telephone call or a short note setting out your story idea will very often produce much better results.

Also of prime importance is that PR practitioners should do their research before contacting a journalist or broadcaster to find out just what he/she writes about or what their programme is all about. *There is the story of the PRO who sent the radio reporter a photograph of a chair for inclusion in his programme*!

USEFUL TIPS

- *It is vital that media questions are handled professionally and competently.*

- *Ensure that all media calls are returned as quickly as possible. Have the correct facts to hand.*

- *Never tell the media **anything** off record.*

- *A 'news' story must be of interest and immediate.*

- *Be clear in your mind what audience you wish to interest and whether your 'news' item is right for that audience.*

- *In general, the following subjects will be of interest to the media: spectacular sales figures, takeover bids, revolutionary new products, job creation.*

- *Careful targeting of the media is required in the PR business – blanket mailing of press releases is not effective PR.*

- *PR practitioners should do their research before contacting journalists to find out what they are writing or broadcasting about.*

5 Setting up and operating the PR office

A comprehensive PR library from which to draw information for the media is a basic requirement for a PRO, and should contain the following:

- Short biographical details and photographs of the general manager, vice-president, chairperson, heads of department/executive staff
- Detailed information describing your organisation/company/product in the form of one, or more, background releases
- Specific press releases relating to individual newsworthy areas of your business
- Photographs to support all releases
- Lists of targeted media contacts including press, TV and radio.

Photographic library

A PR library should contain black-and-white 8" x 6" photographs which can accompany and illustrate the content of your press releases, whether biographical or general.

The extent of the photographic library will depend on the business of your company or organisation. For example, a hotel photographic library should include black-and-white and colour slides of every aspect of the hotel, from the exterior to the bedroom and public areas. If your organisation manufactures consumer products, then your pictures should illustrate all of these. All photographic libraries should contain head-and-shoulder black and white pictures of key personnel within your organisation.

Update your library regularly. Keep track of colour photography requirements.

It is essential that the PRO should use a reliable photographer who can be on call at any time. If in doubt, your local newspaper photographers are often willing to undertake freelance work, and it may well be worth contacting the picture desk at your local paper. The whole area of photography is considered in Chapter 7.

Biographies and how to write them

Biographies and appointment releases should be short and concise. They should be written in the form of a press release, providing facts on the person's working experience, present position and relevant information on awards, hobbies, membership of any relevant professional bodies, marital status and age, although the latter is at the discretion of the person to whom the biography relates.

Extend the biographical details for your executives' local media – they may well be interested in what schools they attended. But take out all these facts when you send the biographical details to your trade, regional or perhaps national media.

Here are two examples of a biographical appointment announcement. Believe it or not, variations on the second version are still being issued to the media by PROs who should know better!

How to do it: specimen biography/appointment release

Top hotelier joins Asia's fastest-growing hotel group

Asia's fastest-growing hotel chain, The Splendid Group, has appointed a top Hong Kong hotelier as manager of its new luxury hotel, the 500-room Hotel Splendid, Kuala Lumpur, Malaysia.

He is 30-year-old David Brown, currently manager of the award-winning Hotel Wonderful, Hong Kong.

The Hotel Splendid Group will have 22 five-star hotels in operation throughout Asia within the next few months, making it one of the biggest in the region.

The Hotel Splendid, Kuala Lumpur, is located in the centre of the city's business and commercial district.

Facilities include an executive floor, complete with library, telex room and secretarial services. There is also a health centre with swimming pool and sauna.

David Brown, a graduate of the highly acclaimed Lausanne Hotel School, Switzerland, has held senior hotel posts throughout the world.

During his time as manager of the Hotel Wonderful, Hong Kong, the establishment won many awards for excellence.

Further information from:
[Contact name, address and
telephone number] [Date]

How **not** to do it: specimen biography/appointment release

Mr David Harold Peter Brown has been appointed to the position of manager of the luxurious new hotel splendid in Kuala Lumper

Mr John Robert Brian Smith, MCIB, HCIT, FNCL, Executive Director of the luxurious new 20-storey, 500-room Hotel Splendid, located in the heart of the fashionable commercial district of Kuala Lumpur, adjacent to the railway station, and Regional Vice-President Kuala Lumpur, Singapore, Bangkok and Hong Kong of the Hotel Splendid Group, which now comprises 12 different luxury, five-star hotels throughout Asia, today announced the appointment of Mr David Harold Peter Brown, formerly Manager of the luxurious 15-storey, 150-room Hotel Wonderful, Hong Kong, as new Manager of the Hotel Splendid, Kuala Lumpur.

Mr David Harold Peter Brown, who is 30 years of age and has been married five times, with 10 children, attended St John's Church of England Primary School in Wigan where he passed the Eleven Plus Examination before moving on to St George's Grammar School, Wigan, where he gained 5 '0' levels, and then attended the Wigan Catering College before going to Lausanne to attend the famous hotel school where he graduated with distinction…

After attending the Lausanne Hotel School Mr David Harold Peter Brown became a kitchen assistant at the Hotel Fleshpot, Soho, London, where after five years he rose to the ranks of sous-chef, before being named sous-chef with the Army Catering Corps, noted for its internationally famous cuisine.

…After serving in various exciting Army locations, Mr David Harold Peter Brown joined the Hotel Wonderful Group, where he held a variety of positions, culminating in his position as Manager of the 150-room Hotel Wonderful, Hong Kong, to which he was appointed on 3rd March and which has since won some awards from newspapers saying that it is excellent.

The Hotel Splendid Group is one of Asia's fastest-growing hotel groups and it plans to open 10 new hotels in the course of the next few months. The Hotel Splendid, Kuala Lumpur, has a hairdressing salon, newspaper kiosk, air-conditioning, an executive floor complete with books, a room for telexes, and where secretaries will lend help, hairdriers in every room, sauna and swimming pool, coffee shop and shoe-shine boys.

Mr John Robert Brian Smith, MCIB, GCIT, FCNL, said today of Mr David Harold Peter Brown:'I'm delighted to appoint Mr David Harold Peter Brown to the position of Manager of the Hotel Splendid, Kuala Lumpur. The Hotel Splendid, Kuala Lumpur, is trying to build a reputation for its cuisine, and I am sure that Mr David Harold Peter Brown, with his experience in the Army Catering Corps, will have a contribution to make in this respect.'

For further information:
[Contact name, address and
telephone number] [Date]

Background releases – the middle ground

A background release is one alternative to the news release. Basically an information sheet filled with facts, it takes a middle ground between the discipline of a news release and a rambling phone call to a reporter or news editor, and is also used to supplement the basic information contained in a short press release.

Below is a brief summary of the type of information that could be included in a background release:

History of the company: The story of your achievements, of the people who have contributed to your development, the growth of your equipment and facilities, a sketch of your financial development and, if relevant, your company's present relationship with the community.

The product: The need it fulfils, how and why it was developed, how it compares with other products, how it is used, and the quality control methods in force.

Manufacturing: The story of the raw materials used and their origins, of the processes and techniques employed, plant facilities and equipment, and the economy and efficiency of the operation.

Marketing and distribution: Marketing methods employed, the extent of the product's distribution, transportation and delivery, unusual outlets, etc.

Research: A description of your laboratory and field facilities, the people engaged in research, your achievements, current developments and future projects, always stressing that research continuously makes products better and cheaper. Attention should be drawn to the work you do in co-operation with technical colleges and universities, government and other industries. The economic and political aspects of the research programme could also be mentioned.

Management: Personality stories about your top management could be prepared with special emphasis on their leadership in one particular field – production, employee relations, research – and on the part they play in local community life.

Welfare: The provisions that you make for employee welfare: canteens, pensions, training, safety, health schemes, further education, etc.

The product in use: A description of the type of people who use your product, equipment or process, where it is used, what it accomplishes and why it is used (such as cost, convenience, superiority, availability, prestige), the volume of use and its growth in popularity.

Preparing a background release can be more difficult than writing a news release because you must try to think of every possible fact, and anticipate every question a reporter may pose. In addition, you should note unusual incidents involved with your event or the subject matter under consideration. Reporters and editors thrive on anecdotes, which can often bring life to an otherwise 'flat' article. Indeed, many feature articles begin with an interesting, unusual or amusing anecdote.

Preparing effective background releases

A loose outline format for backgrounders should begin with the essential information, with supplementary facts and figures added further down the page. If you discover interesting anecdotes, summarise them so the reporter can ask for details. You can also include short, tight 'quotes' that add colour to the story.

Try to keep background releases no longer than two or three pages, though you can attach additional data such as prior news releases, statistics, histories, biographies, diagrams, charts and graphs in an appendix if considered relevant. At all times keep the purpose of the background release in mind: to provide the reporter with *the starting point* for a feature story, or to complement a news release.

A well-prepared background release has the following advantages:

- It provides some control over the content and direction of the story. When a reporter writes a feature, the background release's outline may become the outline for the published piece. This is especially true when a reporter faces a tight deadline

- It can help reduce the chance of errors being printed. This is because you have typed the facts such as names, titles, places and dates, and the reporters concerned can take all this reference material to their desks

- It gives reporters more time to ask substantive questions and follow up on interesting angles, rather than waste valuable time gleaning basic information.

In short, do part of the reporters' job so that they can do a better job with the feature or news story. Your organisation should get a larger, more interesting article in return, and the media will thank you for your foresight. And that could lead to other stories in the future.

Press releases and how to write them

Press or news releases are the greatest bone of contention between PROs and the media because, quite simply, a great many PROs cannot write short, sharp releases. Most of them are far too long and waffle far too much. When you consider that the average trade paper receives in the region of 200 press releases a week (that number plus for the national press each day!) then you realise how competitive it is to get your release noted.

Having said that, releases stand a very good chance of being carried in the trade and local media, including radio, if they are pertinent and well written. Remember, too, that journalists understandably prefer receiving letters addressed to them personally as opposed to the anonymous 'The News Editor', so target your release to a *named* media contact where possible.

Reporters also prefer receiving news releases as opposed to backgrounders for the simple reason that they have insufficient time to write up your story from a string of facts. *In effect, the person writing the press release is doing the writing for the reporter*.

Ideally the article should arrive on the reporter's desk in a style and format the publication can send directly for typesetting. Few releases arrive that way, however, so what characterises those that eventually find their way into print or onto the air, and those that are swept into waste-paper baskets?

The chief reasons for releases not being used are: un-newsworthiness; lack of clarity; lack of detailed facts; and received too late. Thus, a release carrying all the necessary information is more likely to be used and, when used, more likely to be published in a more prominent position than one that doesn't. Reporters are human – despite what some critics would have us believe – and it is understandable that, if faced with a mass of news releases, they are more likely to opt for those containing all the particulars. If they have to phone up to extract even the most basic details, they're more likely to push the release to one side and forget about it.

So, every minute that a public relations person can save a reporter is appreciated and will create better media relations for your organisation.

That doesn't mean, of course, that most newspapers will use press releases verbatim. On the contrary, releases submitted by PROs are frequently 'followed up' by reporters not only to check the facts but often to dig deeper for a new angle to, or elaborate on, an existing angle that particularly interests them. This is especially true of the national media.

Press release style checklist

Newspaper and magazine writing is unlike anything you ever wrote at school or university, unless you studied journalism – and to confuse things even further, every newspaper and magazine has its own style. Thus, writing articles requires training and craftsmanship.

Many news releases are re-written by reporters, so the most important thing is to provide all the facts, clearly and concisely, typewritten, so the reporter can prepare the material for publication.

If, for example, you are dealing with one or two trade papers continually, ask the reporters with whom you will be liaising how they want material presented.

That said, there are several basic principles of copy preparation that most newspapers prefer:

- Type all releases double-spaced or 1.5-line spaced on printed News Release paper if available or on company paper containing the heading 'News Release'. Type on one side of the page only, and leave wide margins on either side. Double-spacing and the margins provide room for sub-editors' alterations and instructions, and typing on only one side prevents half of your story from being lost

- Start the first page with the heading about one-third of the way down. This leaves room for an alternative headline and the sub-editor's typesetting instructions

- At the foot of the sheet include the date in full, the name of the PRO as contact for further information, and the address and telephone number of your organisation

- Limit your release to one or two pages

- Include in the release the name and telephone number (including a home telephone number) of a person to contact for additional information

- Remember the newspaper's deadlines: a 'news' release in the true sense is of no use if it arrives too late

- Make the release newsworthy

- Use simple sentences – and simple words

- Tell the important part of the story first

- Be specific: never use adjectives such as 'fabulous'. Likewise, personal opinions or insinuations should never be part of a press release unless contained within quotes. Give precise measurements or weights rather than simply 'large' or 'heavy'

- Make sure names are spelt correctly; never use initials unless they are in the middle of the name; and include titles after names

- Attribute information to a specific person. It gives more credibility to a story and also adds to its reliability. Avoid, if at all possible, 'A spokesperson said…

- All statements and stories regarding the organisation should be approved by an appropriate authority

- Use brief headings typed in capitals. Spell out numbers up to ten and use numerals for numbers over ten.

How to use a press release

A press release may be used in different ways:

- As a general news story for local newspapers and/or radio and/or television

- As the basis for a feature story, perhaps in combination with a 'backgrounder' release. The news release, once received, may be handed to the features editor who will be expected to investigate the story further and develop a longer article to appear at a later date

- As the basis for press conferences. These are held only to discuss controversial matters or to make special announcements, and consist of single meetings of the media with your organisation's spokesperson(s). Don't organise them unless they are absolutely necessary; press conferences are the ulcer-inducing part of a PRO's life

- As the basis for a media event. Non-controversial yet newsworthy happenings can become the subject of a media event; for example a special function organised solely to obtain publicity, such as company celebrations or milestones or anniversaries. Unless you bring these events to the media's attention they will most likely go unnoticed

- As the basis for a face-to-face interview. A personal interview between a journalist/broadcaster, the PRO and someone from your company will probably have been set up by you. Alternatively, as a result of your release, the editor may have decided that a journalist should conduct a personal interview to discuss the release in more detail.

Developing a rapport with members of the media is the first step in establishing an effective public relations programme. The time spent gaining mutual trust and respect is your investment in future favourable publicity. If you know your media, you will know who is most likely to be interested in the story.

The good and the bad

Here are examples of how to write a press release – and how not to. The first example is how *not* to do it, while the second shows how the professionals tackle the same topic.

*How **not** to do it: specimen press release*

CATCH! Magazine commissions market research survey into fishing and schoolchildren

CATCH! magazine, the exciting and informative partwork series published by Marshall Cavendish for the fishing enthusiast which was launched recently but already attracts a substantial readership, has commissioned marketing researchers Jonathon Bostock to undertake an independent survey into fishing and schoolchildren.

The survey came up with a number of truly interesting and fascinating findings, including the fact that both parents and teachers questioned by the Jonathon Bostock Marketing Research representatives were in agreement that if fishing were introduced into the school curriculum, children would be less likely to become aggressive or indifferent to their environment, while at the same time about 75% of the children interviewed, between the ages of 10 and 16, confirmed to the researchers that they would like to take part in fishing if the activity were introduced as a school subject, whether this took place during school hours or out of school hours.

The survey for CATCH! magazine also came up with the finding that almost half of the children interviewed did fish regularly (reflecting the fact that fishing is one of the fastest growing activities among young people) and while 80% of those were boys (which would seem to confirm the old stereotype), 55% of the children who said they would like to give fishing a try were girls, reasons given for not already fishing being due to a lack of opportunity, rather than a lack of interest.

For all the children who did not already fish, the lack of equipment, fishing companion or opportunity were given as reasons – all problems, surely, which could be solved by organised activity at school?

None of the schools questioned already included fishing on the curriculum, although all were in areas where fishing waters are available, but approximately 80% of schools were in favour of the idea if funds were made available, and all teachers believed that parents would be in favour of fishing being taught, the children, too, confirming that 95% of their parents approved of the idea, with 49% telling the marketing researchers that their mothers and their fathers would much rather them fish than take part in any other sport.

Of the teachers interviewed by the researchers for the CATCH! magazine survey, 75% felt that fishing would improve their pupils' knowledge of the environment, bring them closer to nature and prove to be a calming influence, one teacher telling them, 'It is to be encouraged, it is a quiet, non-aggressive activity, not a 'yobbo' pursuit.'

Finally, the survey findings indicated that the schools would be looking to local authorities to support the cost of fishing lessons.

Further information:
[Name of PR contact] [Date]

How to do it: specimen press release

CATCH! Nets results of fishing survey – could fishing soon be on the school curriculum?

'Gone fishing' could well become a legitimate excuse for schoolchildren according to the results of a survey undertaken by CATCH! magazine.

The CATCH! survey reveals that both parents and teachers are in agreement that if fishing were introduced into the school curriculum, children would be less likely to become aggressive or indifferent to their environment.

And it is evident that the children agree. If fishing were introduced as a school subject, 75% of the children interviewed – aged between 10 and 16 – confirmed that they would like to take part, whether or not this took place during school hours.

Almost half of the children interviewed did fish regularly, reflecting the fact that fishing is one of the fastest growing activities among young people.

While 80% of these were boys – which would seem to confirm the old stereotype -55% of the children who said they would like to give fishing a try were girls. Their reasons for not already participating were due to a lack of opportunity rather than a lack of interest.

The research was undertaken independently by Jonathon Bostock Marketing Research on behalf of CATCH! magazine, a new partwork series for the fishing enthusiast from Marshall Cavendish.

Further information:
[Name of PR contact] [Date]

The effectiveness of the properly constructed press release is illustrated by some of the coverage obtained by it for the Catch! survey.

Part of major coverage obtained from CATCH! survey press release

National TV
BBC TV

National press
The Star

The Mirror

The Daily Express

Radio
Capital Radio

Regional press
Evening Gazette

Sunderland Echo

Belfast News Letter

Express & Star, Wolverhampton

South Wales Argus

Oxford Mail (two items)

Huddersfield Daily Examiner

Ipswich Evening Star

Dudley Evening Mail – Coventry Evening Telegraph (two items)

Birmingham Express and Star

Sandwell Evening Mail

Evening Echo, Southend

Scunthorpe Evening Telegraph

USEFUL TIPS

> *A comprehensive PR library should be set up containing for example, relevant biographies, photographs to support releases, lists of target media.*

> *Update all the information in the PR library on a regular basis.*

> *Biographies and appointments releases should be short and concise.*

> *Background releases or information sheets of no more than two pages, can supplement a short press release. Alternatively, they can provide a journalist with the starting point for a feature.*

> *The key reasons why press releases are not used are: un-newsworthiness, lack of clarity and detailed facts and it was received to late.*

- *A press release should contain all the facts, clearly and concisely, typewritten in double spacing. It should be no more two pages and contain details of a contact for additional information.*

- *A press release may be used as a basis for a news story, feature, press conference or an interview.*

6 Preparing feature articles

Features are a more personalised form of journalism, allowing reporters more creativity than the news side of the media will permit, and thus holding more opportunities for the PRO. Here are some basic principles about placing feature stories:

- Let the newspaper or broadcasting station write the story whenever possible. Even if you have a writer on your staff, the media prefer their own reporters' writing. When journalists put time into a story it is a personal time investment, as well as that of their newspaper's so that resultant articles are much more likely to be used

- A reporter will probably write a longer story, and is likely to think of angles and questions you might omit. More space, of course, usually means a bigger headline and more attention for your company or organisation and its products/services. One possible drawback is that you may lose control of your story. A lengthy news release or feature article presents all the facts in the order you would like them to appear in print, and it may run in a form similar to that which you submitted; this is not so, however, of a reporter-written story. The reporter starts from scratch and all kinds of things may appear in his/her finished article, some of which may even be embarrassing to your organisation or business.

Despite the possible drawbacks, however, this approach is usually worth it. Getting a reporter to consider a story on your company is half the battle; the rest is up to you to see that all the information and comments presented are positive.

Gaining the interest of a particular journalist in writing a feature article about your company or an aspect of its operation is not always possible, so syndicated or one-off feature articles conceived by you 'in house' and submitted to publications or broadcasting stations considered receptive and appropriate can prove an excellent alternative.

If you have an experienced journalist in-house who can undertake this assignment, so much the better. If not, you would be well advised to buy in the services of a journalist with some knowledge and experience of the subject matter involved, and here your trade media is a good source. PR professionals cannot be expected to excel at feature writing – a very specialised form of journalism – so it's always best to have these articles written by people who really know what they are about in terms of journalism and specific knowledge and background on your industry.

In addition to the journalist meeting your chief executive or senior officers to prepare a feature for the newspaper, you may decide to write your own feature, or have your PRO prepare it, for syndication to selected local or regional media.

Feature articles: Case history

Here is a feature article entitled 'Looking for a Job? Don't Snub Hotels and Restaurants', prepared by a PR company some years ago for a trade association in the hotels and restaurants sector to highlight the job and career opportunities within the hotel and catering industries. It was written by a journalist engaged by the PR consultancy for the purpose, and was based on a lengthy meeting he had with the association's chief executive.

The article was used extensively by the media, either whole or as the basis for a follow-up by the various newspapers.

Reproduced here is the letter which accompanied the article and the feature itself, and the media coverage that resulted is also listed.

Specimen letter

Dear Editor,

I have pleasure in enclosing a feature entitled 'Looking for a Job? Don't Snub Hotels and Restaurants.'

You are welcome to use all or part of this feature free of charge.

The theme is particularly topical at this moment as the first Training Board careers seminar of the catering and hotel industry took place in London on October 19. Regional events are being held in Glasgow, Manchester and Birmingham over the next two months.

Also, the first major survey into wages and salaries throughout the hotel and catering industry is due to be published at the end of this month.

I do hope you find it makes interesting reading.

Yours faithfully,

[Name of PR consultant]

Extracts of the specimen feature article

Looking for a job?

Don't snub hotels and restaurants, urges the british hotels, restaurants and caterers association

Local hotels and restaurants are crying out for staff – and hundreds of well-paid, full-time jobs are going begging, according to the British Hotels, Restaurants and Caterers Association.

Robin Lees, the Association's Chief Executive, claims scores of local youngsters are missing out on job opportunities, largely because of poor careers advice in schools.

'The hotel and catering industry, such a vital part of the nation's tourism industry, now employs ten per cent of the 21 million people who make up the British workforce,' he says.

'But the industry is battling against the entrenched attitudes and in-built prejudices of careers officers, teachers and sometimes even parents, who still equate service with servility.

'Hundreds of opportunities exist for the skilled, semi-skilled and unskilled, for school leavers and college graduates. Yet very many of these vacancies remain unfilled because youngsters are being denied, or are failing to capitalise on, the opportunity to get their feet on that crucial first rung of the jobs ladder.'

Mr Lees says that one positive trend is that the campaign his Association has mounted to change the image of the hotel and catering industry and attract more young people – a campaign that includes the staging of local seminars on career prospects in the industry – is working.

'The idea is to get the message over very strongly to 14 year olds in particular that the hotel and catering industry offers tremendous scope. We are doing this by opening up the industry to them and showing them what's available, and taking that through until they are 18 and making their own decisions.'

Mr Lees claims that, nationwide, the hotel and catering industry needs to fill 120,000 vacancies a year, with about 5,000 well-paid jobs going begging in London alone.

He concedes that the industry still has to establish its credibility as the major employer in the UK and as the tourism sector with the greatest growth potential.

'Last year nearly £2 billion was spent on capital investment in major tourism and leisure products in the UK. Of that, an estimated £338 million was invested in new hotels, and over £240 million was spent on hotel expansion and refurbishment – an investment momentum that is the best possible news for jobs.

'By the end of the decade the industry will have created 130,000 new jobs. Our aim is for staff of the right calibre to be drawn into these new jobs.'

Mr Lees says that of the 360,000 school leavers starting a YTS scheme this year only 11,000 entered hotel and catering – although the industry could provide 20,000 places annually.

Entry qualifications for the catering industry vary according to which branch is chosen, but three or four 0-levels are a good start.

'High-flying degree holders and YTS trainees alike can end up as managers within a few years if they show they have natural aptitude, and the possibilities for promotion and advancement are limitless.'

Mr Lees admits that the salaries of between £50,000 and £60,000 per year earned by top chefs in some of the country's most famous restaurants and hotels are very much the exception rather than the rule, but says salaries within the industry are by no means as poor as critics sometimes claim.

Mr Lees says the BHRCA has been working closely with bodies such as the Hotel and Catering Training Board in the provision of better training programmes for new entrants to the industry, including the staging of a series of seminars held in key centres throughout the country.

It is also stepping up its efforts to increase knowledge within schools and colleges of the career opportunities available in the industry.

'It only remains to convince school leavers and young people that the industry is a worthwhile one to enter, and that it offers them excellent career prospects and good salaries if they are prepared to train and work.'

Further press information from:
[Name of PR contact and telephone number]
[Date]

Hotels and restaurants article: media response

National media

The Daily Mail

The Guardian

The Times

The Daily Telegraph

The Daily Express

The Daily Mail

'The Jimmy Young Programme'

Regional media

The Evening Sentinel, Stoke-on-Trent

Bath & West Evening Chronicle

Evening Herald, Plymouth

Eastern Daily Press

Eastern Evening News

Reading Evening Post

Evening Advertiser

Dorset Evening Echo

Evening Chronicle, Oldham

The Western Morning News

Evening Post, Kent

Express & Echo, Exeter

City of London Post

Glasgow Herald

East Anglian Daily Times

Evening Gazette, Middlesbrough

The Star, Sheffield

The Doncaster Star

MS London

Trade media

Caterer & Hotelkeeper

Personnel in Management

Travel News (now *Travel Weekly*)

Catering South West

USEFUL TIPS

- *Let the newspaper or broadcasting station write the story wherever possible – the media prefer their own reporters' writing.*

- *Getting a reporter to consider a story on your company or product is half the battle; the rest is up to you to see that all the information and comments presented are positive.*

- *If you are unable to interest a journalist in writing a feature about your company/product, consider buying in the services of a journalist with some knowledge and experience of the subject matter involved.*

> *Get your in-house journalist to write a syndicated or one-off feature article based on your in-house ideas. Submit the article to media who are considered receptive and appropriate.*

7 Public relations photography

One photograph, it is said, can be worth a thousand words. While the claim may sound something of an exaggeration, there is no denying the tremendous PR value of photographs. Photographs stimulate interest. Editors position photographs in their publications to give visual impact.

Finding a photographer

The first step is for you to have access to a few reliable local photographers who can be on call at any time. As local newspaper photographers are often willing to undertake freelance work, contact the picture desk at your local paper. Be careful about using one-person outfits; if you have to meet a deadline, it is of little value employing a photographer who will be unable to process the pictures until the following day because of his/her work schedule. The PRO of a large non-competitive company may let you have the name of his/her photographer, as will a local hotel with photographers for their conference clients. *Hollis PR Directory* has a section on PR photographers/photographic companies covering the country. Try out the photographers on in-house jobs before any major PR event.

Photo opportunities

When approaching a newspaper editor or reporter with a story idea, bring up some photo suggestions too; your visual idea may be rejected but you will get a feel for what type of pictures they prefer and it may even spark off another photo possibility which the newspaper *will* use. However, it is important to remember that while magazines and trade publications will use your PR photographs, most regional and national newspapers will want to take their own photographs and use their own photographers. All they will require from the PR department is convincing that a photo opportunity exists.

PR professionals, quite rightly, often spend hours of time working on 'photo opportunities'. Why? Because readers almost always notice photos, and that means the caption and accompanying article stand a better chance of being read; even if they merit only a cursory glance, you have gained more attention value than you would have done with a printed story alone. Do not, however, get carried away. Study the photographs used in your local media or in the nationals and you will see that very seldom do they blatantly 'plug' a product; that is left to the trade press. The photo idea must involve more than just an opportunity for you to plug your product. The skill is being able to incorporate the product either by the photo telling the whole story or the photo stimulating the recipient to read on.

If you are supplying the photographs remember to check whether the publication requires black-

and-white, colour prints or transparencies. For many years, colour reproduction in magazines required a colour transparency but nowadays new printing technology is moving towards the colour print.

Remember, press photographers are under no obligation to turn up to your photo-call – the picture/news desk may put them on a potentially better story at the last moment – so you must always have your own photographer present.

Your own photographer should be one of the first people you consult regarding a photo-call. Ask them how they would present the event photographically, discuss options and props. After all, they will know your product and the image you wish to project. They can advise you on the technical side of the photographic session; also your photographer can take the shots you want – the press may not.

If for any reason there is a safety aspect to the venue (hard-hat or no-smoking area, eye protection, etc), then be sure to hold a briefing session, both with your own colleagues and invited journalists/photographers to this effect prior to the taking of any photographs.

However, placing a photo in a newspaper or magazine is difficult for several reasons. First, most newspapers employing a photographic staff want to take their own pictures. The few non-staff photos used include agency wire shots (from AP, UPI, etc), 'mug shots' of executives in the business pages and – rarely – a publicity photo set up by a corporate PR department or PR consultancy. Enquire of those journalists turning up without their staff photographer if your own photographer can take an exclusive shot for their publication.

Then there is the lack of space. Photographic space is even more at a premium than space for words and there is considerable competition for it, so it is essential to use creative thinking if you hope to interest a newspaper in accepting and publishing one of your pictures, or sending their own staff photographer to take a picture.

Here are some tips to help you gain the most out of photo opportunities:

- The idea has to be good. Some stories have natural visual aspects, and the job of a good PR person is to bring these to the attention of a reporter or editor. As in all aspects of PR, don't waste the media's time

- Planning is essential. You might have to create both a photo opportunity and convince people in your organisation that photos are worth their time and trouble. You may find yourself having to carry heavy props to a site convenient for a photographer. Sometimes, the photographer's schedule will not match your chairperson's schedule, so diplomacy and patience will be needed to achieve what you want

- Dreaming up photo possibilities is more difficult than you imagine. Don't be too blinkered. Be sure to involve the person in charge of the project and if necessary 'brainstorm' ideas: have everyone submit suggestions while you note them. What you want are the unusual, or the incongruous, visual ideas. Prepare props in advance

- It is also important to treat the photographer on an equal footing with a journalist: introduce them to the chairperson, guest of honour, etc. Often the photographs of the PR event are 'for the record', and no more. A good photographer will have special 'exclusive' requirements from your event; pay attention to them. A positive move is to meet with your local newspaper or trade photographer and have a general discussion on how to help get the best out of your PR event. Find out what sort of picture they will run with

- Even if you have all the press turning out, you *must* still have the first photo planned. If it is good, the photographers will expand on the idea, otherwise they will quickly shoot it before moving on to their own ideas. A useful rule is to ensure your 'cast' are doing something: an action photograph is far better than a static photograph.

A few don'ts:

- Organisations and companies love photos of their officers shaking hands, probably with a chief guest. Newspapers, on the whole, do not. If you convince a hard-boiled newspaper photographer to attend your meeting/launch with only a handshake as a photo subject you will lose ground in your media relations

- Likewise, the standard group photo is seldom interesting to anyone but those in the photo. Unless the photographer directs you to do something else, pose a small, selective group in an unusual setting. Remember the cardinal rule: *newspapers want picture-orientated subjects*, things that are unusual, good graphically, and tell a story by themselves. As a general rule, they do not like big groups of people, but much prefer two or three people in an animated and lively pose. This latter point applies to a number of trade publications.

Plan the photographic event carefully, considering interesting action shots you can suggest, and prepare your people to co-operate. The golden rule is to be punctual; photographers run on very tight schedules, and they usually allow no more than 15 minutes leeway for assignments. If your senior executives are late or you haven't got your act together, press photographers are unlikely to hang around until you are ready. They will move on to the next appointment. Stress this important point to the central figures of your 'show', the chairperson for example. They will often say their time is more important than the media's. If they take this attitude it is fairly certain you will miss out on some valuable media coverage.

The time of day of your function is also an important factor – particularly in winter when 'photographic daylight' is at a premium: photographers often want to shoot outside. Allow time for processing prints if you wish to meet a deadline.

How to present the photograph

The photograph has been taken; now to present it properly.

An 8" x 6" photograph is usually the best size to use. Caption all copies of the photograph as follows:

- Type double-spaced, double-lined with wide margins on the lower half of a sheet of News Release paper, the date, location, names of people, their positions in the company and any other specific details, eg release/embargo date, contact name with 24-hour phone number, etc

- Lightly glue the four corners of the photograph onto the paper above the caption

- In case of a lengthy caption, stick the picture on the reverse of the sheet

- Identify people by their full names and titles from left to right.

- Alternatively, if you are providing the image on disc, check that you save it on an agreed format.

Finally, remember that photographers attend PR events every day of the week, every week of the year. The more you plan and prepare the shoot, including providing props, the more co-operation you will get from the photographers who will then be fighting on your side to get the photo used by their picture editors.

USEFUL TIPS

- Don't underestimate the value of photographs in PR.

- Access a few reliable local photographers who can be on call the whole time.

- Plan and prepare your photo opportunity well: ensure that the idea is good and that the timing is right for the media.

- Picture editors want picture-orientated subjects: things that are unusual, good graphically and tell a story in themselves.

- Always have your photographer present at your photo opportunity.

- Magazine and trade publications may well use your PR photographs, but most regional and national media will want to take their own photographs.

- If you are supplying the photographs, check in which format they are required: print, transparency or on disc.

> *Ensure that the correct details are sent out with the photograph (date, location, names of people, embargo date, contact number).*

8 Press conferences, media events and interviews

In this chapter we look at meeting the media.

Press conferences

A press conference is an effective means of publicising to the media an important development within your company or organisation, but the pros and cons need to be considered carefully before you decide to go ahead with this particular PR approach. Journalists generally prefer 'exclusive' stories whenever possible, but if you have a major announcement to make, a press conference is an efficient way of doing so. Economics these days make press conferences an expensive business, especially if paying for rooms or hotels is involved, so only have a press conference if your news is vital or if you feel that, once a year, your senior executives should meet the media for a mutually beneficial exchange of ideas and thinking. If this is the case, then be honest with the media and say they are being invited for an 'update briefing'.

If you do decide to arrange a press conference, follow these guidelines:

- When to schedule? Check that the date does not coincide with another major press conference or local media event. Get in touch with the news editor of the local newspaper or radio/television station, or your contacts on the national or trade press; they should be able to advise on any conflict in times

- Who to invite? Invite the news editors of all media in your area including any special interest magazines. They will allocate an available journalist. Also invite, personally, your own media contacts. Local dignitaries or officials and other community opinion leaders should also be invited if appropriate. But remember, it is media publicity you are seeking, so the media and its requirements should come first. The other danger in inviting local dignitaries or officials is that the media may uncover another and perhaps better story or angle which could overshadow what your people have to say. Issue printed invitations – or personally addressed, and signed, letters of invitation – in plenty of time. If the conference is designed to produce a 'news story', make the letter as enticing as possible without going overboard.

Specimen letter of invitation

[Date]

[Address]

Dear

Happy Holidays launches 2000 programme – Tuesday, 16 February 1993

Happy Holidays, the UK's leading domestic tour operator, has expanded its 1994 summer programme by 30%.

I should be pleased if you can attend a press conference on Tuesday, 16 September 1999 where John Smith, Managing Director, Happy Holidays, will be revealing full details of the new programme and discussing the strategy behind it.

The conference will start at 12.30 for 1.00 pm at the Holiday Inn Mayfair, Berkeley Square, London, W1. It will be followed by a buffet lunch and the opportunity to meet other key Happy Holidays executives including Joe Bloggs, Finance Director, and Tom Brown, Sales and Marketing Manager.

If you have any further queries, please do not hesitate to call me or my colleague, Louise White. Our direct line is…

I do hope you will be able to join us on the 16th and look forward to seeing you.

Yours sincerely

[Name]

[Title]

- Two days before the event, telephone those who have not replied and compile a list of acceptances. Watch the timing of this call. It will irritate the media if you ring about the reply just when they are going to press. Research the best time to ring your media: in the morning or late afternoon?

- Prepare a typed outline of the form the conference is to take, and present it to the media on arrival. Don't make the kit too bulky; it is not necessary to include every item of publicity material from your organisation, only that which is relevant

- Ask attendees to sign or rather *print* their name in a visitor's book so that you have a record of who attended, and, equally important, who did not, so you can arrange for the information to be sent or delivered to the absentees by messenger as soon as possible but check whether they require it – you may be wasting your time and money

- Prepare a press release which details the subject of the press conference, and include this in a press kit which should be distributed on arrival

- Arrange speakers at a table on a dais with large cards in front of them clearly indicating their name and title

- Ensure that the media briefing is short and to the point

- If radio and television coverage is required, discuss the facilities needed in advance of the day. Make sure a visual identity of the organisation's name is placed in such a way that the cameras cannot help but pick it up and give you valuable free publicity, eg a company banner/sign behind the dais where the speakers are sitting. This is used most effectively these days by hotels when press conferences are televised

- Embargoes. You may wish to give your story in advance to a contact who cannot attend your conference. An embargo means that the media should not print or broadcast your story until after the time you have stipulated, eg 1.00 pm if your conference is set for 12.30 for 1.00 pm. Very rarely has the media broken an embargo – until recently. Sadly, because of circulation wars and the breakdown of the 'unwritten rule' principle, many newspapers are now breaking embargo deadlines. So be careful – you really can't trust the media, at least in this area.

Media events

This is an informal gathering of the media to cover an event staged by your company or organisation, such as a celebration or anniversary, where, for example, local newspaper photographers are invited to capture the event.

Invitations must be sent to news editors of local papers, radio and television stations, and it is also advisable to send an invitation to the picture editors of the local newspapers since it is they who control

SECTION EIGHT

the staff photographers and decide which photographs will be used in the newspapers.

A news release should be given to all media, including the photographers, on their arrival. This should give details of the event, the organisers, and any other relevant information.

Face-to-face interviews

Face-to-face interviews are among the best means available of obtaining good media coverage, and are generally much more effective than large-scale press gatherings. This is because, as indicated earlier, journalists, especially news editors, prefer 'exclusive' stories and angles wherever possible, and are much more likely to 'spike' or play down stories which they know other newspapers have also been given (unless, of course, the story is so sensational and important that they would be failing in their duty to their readers by not reporting it in full).

Many journalists will not ask their most important questions at a conference in front of their competitors for fear, quite rightly, of giving away their own particular 'angle' and will often seek out a face-to-face interview immediately after the formal press conference; so be prepared. Since most companies' stories are not earth-shattering, face-to-face interviews will generally produce better results, and if the right reporter from the 'right' newspaper or magazine – that is, the medium in which coverage of your company would be most advantageous – is invited, excellent results can be achieved.

It is also worth remembering that important local or trade media may merit a private briefing, embargoed, before that major press conference.

Once the particular newspaper/journalist has been identified for the face-to-face briefing, the following guidelines should be applied:

- The PRO should be familiar with the publication/radio/television programme the journalist works for and its type of readership/audience. If a radio or TV station wishes to conduct a live interview it is quite acceptable to ask the journalist involved the nature of the interview and what questions are likely to be asked. In this way the PRO can research the answers to be given by the interviewee

- Make sure a positive message is included within the written news release, which should be given to the journalist before the interview is undertaken

- Use notes on the subject under discussion; do not rely on memory. Give the journalist a full press kit before the interview so that all the facts are to hand.

Press lunches

Hosting a media lunch can be an excellent way, apart from a press conference, of announcing news and giving updated information on your product, and especially effective if it is an informal occasion that gives both press and the company/organisation the chance to discuss points of mutual interest face-to-face.

However, it is important to remember that the last thing most journalists need is yet another free lunch – most are inundated with lunch invitations every day – so the letter of invitation must include details of the reason for holding the event, such as the story to be discussed, and indicate that the event will give the media the opportunity to question the client directly. The letter of invitation, in fact, is of paramount importance, since it can stimulate a news editor's or journalist's interest, or do the opposite. Great care and thought should be given to its composition, therefore, in order to create an aura of interest and importance to the planned event and thus provoke a firm acceptance.

In order to maintain a well-balanced client/media guest list, it is advisable not to exceed, say, ten press and three client representatives who are of management status.

Media lunches are best arranged in a private room of a restaurant or hotel. All media representatives should be given a press kit on arrival, giving details of what is to be announced. Lunch is normally preceded by cocktails/open bar, and is an ideal time for both client and media to meet.

Speeches are best delivered before lunch, allowing the actual time during lunch for continuing discussions, and for the media to leave early if they wish.

Ensure that the timing of the event is punctual; do not allow it to run on until late afternoon, since this will only irritate and inconvenience the journalists. A suggested timetable could be: 12.30 Drinks, 12.55 Speech, 1.00 Lunch, 2.30 Finish.

Whoever is making the speech should be briefed by the PRO beforehand on what 'angle' the journalists are most likely to be interested in, what things to avoid saying or to play down, what awkward questions might be asked, and the appropriate replies to them.

It is advisable to rehearse a 'question and answer' session with your executives in advance. Think of and plan the answers to all the negative questions.

Media visits

Hosting a media group requires a great deal of personal time, involvement and patience on the part of the PR officer. But the benefits of this kind of PR activity are numerous, the most obvious being that you have a group of journalists as a captive audience, comparatively ready and willing to be given stories and news for as long as they are your guests. It is, therefore, vital that their visit is planned and co-ordinated with meticulous detail.

Whether the journalists are being invited to view your hotel, experience your country, see the manufacture of a new electronic product, or attend the opening of a new factory for two days or five, the organisation of their visit should be based on the same concept, and the same basic rules applied.

First, decide why it would be beneficial for you to invite a number of the media at one time. What story do you have to tell that is best experienced at first hand by the writer, rather than told in the form of a press release or feature article?

Decide which category of media you wish to reach and research the names of the relevant correspondents who might be interested in writing about your product. If they are regular media contacts of yours then your job is easier; if not, you should write to the editor of the publication suggesting that they may wish to nominate a representative to participate in the visit.

It is important that any media group is kept small – the ideal number is six, with ten as the maximum – in order that each can receive personal attention from you.

In the official letter of invitation outline the purpose of the visit and the itinerary, and indicate dates and the duration of their stay. If at this stage you can confirm their travel arrangements, give details; otherwise it is acceptable to supply these later.

The PRO should be prepared to be present with the group at all times, unless specified in the itinerary. It is also important to ensure that the schedule includes details of when the journalists will be expected to pay their own expenses. This usually occurs during free time when appointments are not scheduled.

Include in the itinerary details of all official appointments, breakfasts, lunches and dinners that will be hosted by your organisation or other officials. Give details of times when you require the presence of the journalists and indicate where and when particular codes of dress are required.

As an additional aid, it is always helpful to advise on the local temperatures, especially if journalists are visiting from overseas, so that they can adjust their wardrobe requirements.

Media visit checklist

Do:

- Keep the size of your group to a number that can be easily handled by you

- Make sure the itinerary is an interesting combination of work and pleasure

- Be prepared to be on duty 24 hours a day. Journalists like to think they have the right to call on your advice at any time, and invariably do!

Do not:

- Plan a media visit that lasts five days when the itinerary can be accomplished comfortably in three

- Waste journalists' time. If they cannot think of anything to do during their free time, advise them of the interesting options

- Do not overload the itinerary. Remember that the media are human!

USEFUL TIPS

- *Journalists generally prefer 'exclusive' stories whenever possible, but if you have a major announcement to make, a press conference is an efficient way of doing so.*

- *Brief your speakers prior to the event and prepare an informative press kit. Make sure that the media briefing is short and to the point.*

- *Face-to-face interviews are one of the best and generally most effective ways of obtaining good media coverage.*

- *Important local or trade media may merit a private briefing, embargoed, before your major press conference. Always give the journalist a full press kit before the interview so that all the facts are to hand.*

- *At press lunches it is not advisable to exceed, say, ten press and three client representatives who are of management status.*

- *Plan any media visits with meticulous detail – they can be an ideal opportunity to have a group of journalists as a captive audience.*

> *Keep the size of your group on a media visit to a manageable size so that each journalist can receive your personal attention. Make sure the itinerary is an interesting combination of work and pleasure.*

9 Be effective on radio or television

In these days of media hype, trial by television and the radio phone-in, confidence and ability in front of the media's cameras and microphones have become extremely valuable assets for the aspiring manager, and for the person already at the top.

Since natural ability in this medium is rare, the techniques must be learned, and the good PR practitioner should be adept at passing on tips to both the upwardly mobile and established manager alike.

What should be remembered from the outset is that the electronic media are there for you to use, to talk about your factory, your profession, your business or whatever. It is 'free' publicity, and when you consider the sky-high costs of television commercials, especially at peak viewing times, an interview, which costs you nothing but your time, must be infinitely better value.

Even if the media wants to talk to you because something has gone wrong in your company or business, you can nearly always turn that bad news into good news, just as long as you know what you are doing.

But broadcasting is not plain sailing. You must realise, for instance, that the interviewer's aim for an interview and yours are not necessarily – indeed are seldom – the same. The former's objective is to create interesting television, while yours is to get your message across, which means that to achieve your aim you must make your message good television or radio.

Remember you are both using the same article, and the shortage of time is your biggest problem: you will never have enough time when you are being interviewed.

On television, the average interview lasts between 2-4 minutes, and for a minute of that the interviewer is talking, so you will have about 90 seconds to tell your story or get your message across. Even if you are interviewed for half an hour the chances are that only a couple of minutes of it will be broadcast; the rest will be edited out.

Media interview techniques

So, what are the important points to bear in mind about media interview techniques? The first thing is to make the most of the limited time at your disposal, because the basic premise for giving an interview on television or radio is that it is about saying what you've gone there to say… it is not a courtroom cross-examination and therefore you are under no obligation to go along with the interviewer's line of questioning.

It goes without saying that you must find out, either directly or through your PR consultant, what you are letting yourself in for; often it is your only chance to avoid becoming involved in something very unhelpful, such as a programme which turns out to be anti the business you represent. Unless you ask in advance you could find that you and your company are used as the prime examples, simply because you agreed to take part. You need to ask a lot of questions before you accept an invitation to broadcast.

You also need to remember that 90 per cent of the work of an interview takes place before you leave your office, which means taking time to prepare your message, with PR assistance, and reduce it to something you can say in 90 seconds.

As well as deciding on what you are going to say, you also have to decide what you are not going to say, because there are bound to be subjects you do not want to discuss on air.

Furthermore, if there is a skeleton lurking in your cupboard you have to assume the interviewer knows about it. You must, therefore, be quite clear in your mind what you are going to do if it is brought up – which in most cases means changing the subject! Watch and study politicians when asked direct questions. They seldom answer the question posed, especially if it is a 'difficult' one (in other words, one they prefer not to answer), but they turn the question round to answer an unspoken one they are prepared to answer.

It is not only the aggressive interviewer who can give you a problem – uninformed interviewers, of which alas there are many, are just as dangerous, because silly questions can provoke silly answers if you are not careful.

To broadcast successfully, you have to apply four basic rules: keep it simple, make it personal, quote examples and describe things visually.

The best communicators often use analogies to illustrate significant points. Labour politician Dennis Healey, interviewed on breakfast television talking about the EEC's refusal to impose sanctions on South Africa, said: 'The Danish Prime Minister complained the motion had been amputated. It was more than amputated; in the morning Chancellor Kohl cut off the arms and legs and in the afternoon Mrs Thatcher kicked the torso in the teeth!' He painted a vivid picture of the destruction of an ideal which sticks in the memory.

There are, of course, numerous occasions when you may be called upon to give an interview on radio or television:

- To answer a complaint or query from a member of the public on a live radio phone-in programme
- To give information on a matter involving your company or organisation on a news or current affairs programme
- To join a discussion group on a subject which concerns or affects your company or industry, perhaps on a current affairs programme.

Checklist: effective interviews

Here, then, is a list of hints and tips to help you get the most out of a radio or television interview:

- Don't be scared – be prepared. When invited to appear, *ask* and note down:
  - Who's calling; the company; phone number; subject; programme; interviewer; when; where; is it live?
  - Why me/us?
  - Who else is involved?
  - Will they be showing any visuals?
  - Most important of all: give yourself time to think before accepting

- Prepare:
  - Your message: three points maximum, reduced to simple statements. Never write down your answers word-for-word and read them; you are holding a conversation with an interviewer, not reading a statement
  - Your response to all difficult questions
  - Your change-of-direction phrases to control the course of the interview

- Don't think about who may be listening. Pretend that you and the interviewer are alone and that what you have to tell them is the most important thing they will have ever heard. After all, you are being interviewed because you have information which they want to hear

- When you are speaking, don't talk too quickly. Relax, take your time and speak distinctly. Don't mumble or slur your words
 - Avoid technical terms, professional jargon and organisation slang. Figures and statistics should be kept to a minimum but if you must use figures, always round them off. Too short an answer may give the impression that you are trying to be too smart. Too long an answer is hard to follow and often becomes boring. Just try to say what you have to say in as clear and concise a manner as possible

- Try to avoid verbal mannerisms such as 'you know', 'at this point in time', 'well, I believe', and 'and so on'
- At the interview you will always be short of time, so ensure you:
    - Make your point(s) at the beginning
    - Stick to your own subject. Don't waste time on digressions
    - Jump on untruths. Interrupt if necessary
    - Are positive throughout
    - Mention your company or product (if appropriate) at the beginning, middle and end so that if the interview is cut your product still stands a chance of being referred to
- Never say: 'No comment. I am unable to confirm or deny.' This often makes it appear

that you are confirming whatever it is that the interviewer is asking you. Instead it is better to try variations of 'A full investigation is taking place… ' or 'I don't yet know but…' After you have effectively said 'No comment' you can then say what you want to say. Be careful about appearing to avoid a question. If you are really on the spot it is probably best to be honest and say you don't know

- If you are answering a question 'live', that is directly 'on air', do not be afraid to pause and think before you speak. Do not panic if you become tongue-tied or if the interviewer is giving you a difficult time; just take a deep breath and try to remain cool. If it is possible, have a brief chat with the interviewer before you actually start recording so that you have some idea of what questions are likely to be asked

- Never lose your temper, shout or be rude. Always remain polite and calm, but don't allow yourself to be intimidated by an overbearing interviewer or fellow interviewee

- If you are being interviewed face-to-face in your own office, make sure you are comfortable. Sit where you want to sit unless it is necessary to move for technical reasons

- Don't grab hold of the microphone when you are talking. The interviewer or sound recordist will make sure it is in the best position for your voice

- If the interview is pre-recorded, by all means ask to have it played back. If you are not satisfied you can ask to do all, or part of it, again. If you don't think you can improve on the first effort then just leave it. This, of course, is in an ideal world. My advice is that once you have recorded the interview, it is highly unlikely that an interviewer would agree to do it all over again – unless *all* parties agreed that it was best to do so

- In order to put across your message effectively, you must:
  - Keep it simple and jargon free
  - Make it personal, by using personal pronouns
  - Make it interesting by giving examples
  - Make it memorable by describing things visually and using analogies

- There is nothing to be nervous about, unless you have something to hide. In that case it would perhaps be better not to give an interview. Many people are more nervous about giving a radio interview than talking to a reporter with a notebook; in fact, you are in more danger of being misquoted by someone who has to read back his notes than by a microphone which you have actually spoken into.

Interview training

Remember, the electronic media is there to be used, and you should be out there using it. But remember, too, that only fools rush in where angels fear to tread. So first find out how to do it.

There are a number of courses available. These can be conducted either internally, aimed at senior executives and run by a professional radio and television interviewer, or at public courses which can attract up to 60 delegates.

Almost all of the well-known radio or TV broadcasters are available – at a price – to undertake detailed sessions for companies. Most popular are people like Peter Hobday and Douglas Cameron who are particularly good at giving an insight into the workings of radio.

For senior executives, a private course for a select few to minimise embarrassment is recommended. All courses include television equipment, cameras and playback facilities.

The private tuition on the successful handling of radio and TV interviews is not cheap, but an effective three-minute interview given by your marketing director can be invaluable to the sales of a product.

Finally, take heart. As Peter Hobday says: 'We do not want a frightened incoherent chief executive on our programmes. It is not our intention to embarrass him, so if he is positive, confident, knows his facts and can respond to us succinctly, then that makes our programme interesting.'

USEFUL TIPS

- *You can nearly always turn bad news into good news, just as long as you know what you are doing.*

- *The broadcaster's objective is to create interesting television/radio, while yours is to get your message across, which means that to achieve your aim you must make your message good television or radio.*

- *Make the most of your limited time – you have about 90 seconds to get your message across.*

- *Before you commit yourself to a broadcast interview, ask a lot of questions, either directly or through your PR consultant.*

- *Prepare your message (three points maximum) and know in advance what you are going to say and what you are not going to discuss on air.*

- *Always prepare your response to difficult questions and become familiar with change of direction phrases to control the course of the interview.*

> *Arrange tuition on the successful handling of radio and television interviews for yourself and/or appropriate senior executives.*

> *To broadcast successfully you need to: keep it simple, make it personal, quote examples and describe things visually.*

10 PR on a small budget

In PR, as in most other things, as I said earlier, you get what you pay for. A PR budget of only £5,000 a year, for instance, certainly won't go very far: it will not cover the cost of engaging the services of a full-time secretary, let alone a skilled PR practitioner, whereas companies with £30,000+ to spend can expect a good degree of professional PR expertise for their money.

But even if budget restrictions do not allow you to employ an in-house PR professional or an outside consultancy, you can still make use of PR techniques to promote your company, association or product, whether it be a small hotel or a national charity.

Tips on how to do so are scattered throughout this book. However, since I realise that many companies and organisations face the dilemma of wanting to operate PR but with very small funds at their disposal, here are some basic steps. To make the guidelines more relevant, the requirements of a small, town-centre hotel are used as an illustration, but of course most of the principles can be applied to most service sectors, such as retail outlets, and can be adapted by a variety of small businesses.

The hotel scenario

Know your market

It is absolutely no use trying to implement a PR plan unless you know the market for which you are catering and the market you are out to satisfy. If your hotel is patronised almost exclusively by travelling salespeople, and you are quite happy to stay with this market but would like to expand it further, there would be no point promoting your hotel extensively within the immediate neighbourhood. Instead, the PR effort should be directed at the travelling salespeople who do not already know of your hotel's existence and the facilities it can offer them.

This can be done through magazines devoted to the sales and marketing sectors of the community, and through the business/commerce columns of national newspapers.

It could well be, on the other hand, that while occupancy rates at your hotel during the week are excellent, the place practically 'dies' at the weekends when the business guests are not around. In this case you either need to encourage business guests to stay on over the weekend, either by introducing low-price weekend breaks, or attract the leisure market to fill the empty rooms from Friday to Monday.

Why your product?

Once you have established the market you want your PR to reach, it is important to appraise your product honestly, and determine its strengths and weaknesses – in particular any *unique selling points*

(USPs). Very few aspects of life, of course, are unique, but if you take a good, long look at your product you should be able to come up with some plus points that distinguish it from the competition.

Talk to your regular guests, and find out from them why they prefer using your hotel to the one down the road.

Is it, for example, because your room rates are lower than the competition's, your bar is the liveliest in town, the facilities you offer the business guest are particularly good (specific writing surfaces in bedrooms, together with trouser presses, tea/coffee making facilities), or is your restaurant the best locally?

Whatever the reasons, once you have established them, you are well on the way to being able to instigate a PR action plan.

PR action plan

Having determined the market you are seeking and the USPs you believe should do the trick, make yourself familiar with the media which could be useful to you, whether it be business press, sales/marketing magazines, local radio, women's magazines or whatever. The reference section of your local library should have directories giving not only complete listings of the media but circulation figures, copy deadlines etc; there are also specialist directories available.

Step two is to create a PR angle that is likely to interest the targeted media, based on your hotel's USPs. If, for example, the best thing about your hotel is its restaurant, in which you are employing, at vast expense, a very bright and innovative young chef, your target media will not only be your local newspapers and radio stations, to encourage more local diners, but also specialist food writers from the national media, particularly the up-market magazines. Getting your restaurant mentioned in a publication such as *Vogue, Harper's & Queen* or one of the credit card companies' glossies such as Diner's Club's *Signature* can ensure its success for years.

So how do you create a PR angle that might interest the media in your restaurant? Simply inviting a representative of the target media to come and sample a meal is not enough; indeed, since food writers are inundated with invitations to try the thousands of new restaurants constantly springing up in all parts of the country, an invitation from you, unless given the PR treatment, is quite likely to fall by the wayside.

The answer is to make the restaurant seem excitingly different, either in ambience or food or, preferably, both. If it specialises in English food, for example, get the chef to introduce a range of unusual dishes culled from an ancient recipe book, or dishes which are peculiar to the area in which your hotel is located. In other words, be creative and innovative about the aspects of your product you believe are worth highlighting, and you stand a much better chance of enticing the media, if for no other reason than that the ancient recipes of unusual dishes will give the journalist an angle for his/her story.

The above is a very simple example of basic PR which can be achieved at very little cost, except in time. And the same basic principles apply whatever is being marketed or promoted.

PR done skillfully is an expensive and time-consuming practice, but one which can, and does, produce excellent results. There is absolutely no reason that the basic PR principles cannot be applied by small businesses which simply do not have the money.

The writing of a press release, for example, is an acquired skill, and badly written ones can do more harm than good. Engaging the services of a local freelance journalist to write them on your behalf is a sensible option. He or she may even waive a cash fee for the exercise in return for a couple of elaborate meals in your restaurant!

There is no great myth or mystique to public relations – it is basically a matter of common sense, doing your homework, and then being realistic about what you hope to achieve, and how you are going to achieve it.

USEFUL TIPS

- *Know the market for which you are catering and the market you are out to satisfy.*

- *Appraise your product – honestly – and determine its strengths and weaknesses. In particular look at the unique selling points (USPs).*

- *Make yourself familiar with the media who could be useful to you (the library should have directories giving media listings, circulation figures, copy deadlines etc).*

- *Develop a PR angle that might interest the media – be creative and innovative.*

- *Badly written press releases can do more harm than good so, if necessary, engage the services of a local freelance journalist to write them on your behalf.*

- *PR is basically a matter of common sense: prepare well and be realistic about what you hope to achieve and how it is to be done.*

11 New product launches

The same basic guidelines apply no matter what you are launching, whether it be a restaurant, a magazine or a new car.

Launch theme and date

Decide on a theme for the launch. This could involve a special venue, date, number, colour, dish, costume etc. It could also mean having to hire special equipment or book personalities. But remember that the media are interested in a *story*, so do not go to great lengths for a theme for the media and forget to create an interesting, newsworthy story for them.

When deciding on a date for the launch, ensure that:

- The chief executives of the company will be available
- The date does not clash with a similar launch or other major media event
- The most important media representatives are likely to attend.

Obviously no date will suit everyone, so after taking the above precautions it is best to settle on a date as soon as possible.

Venue

Make sure:

- The cost of the venue is within the company's budget
- It is a reasonable size for the number of people you expect to attend
- That, if at all possible, it is in a central location convenient for the majority of the guests.

Refreshments

- Decide whether a meal or refreshments will be offered, and who will provide them
- Give caterers an indication of numbers. (These can be finalised nearer the time of the event.)

Guest list and invitations

- Invite all media who are likely to be interested in the launch, not just the obvious ones
- Try finding out the names of specific journalists in advance to avoid having to address invitations to the editor, the news editor, etc
- Produce printed invitations to be sent out, if possible, three weeks in advance
- After a week to ten days, telephone those who have not replied and compile a list of acceptances
- On the day before the event, telephone all invitees as a final reminder.

Photography

- Book a photographer to take both colour and black-and-white pictures of the launch which can be offered to the media.

Client briefing

- Make sure that the client or chief executive knows exactly what is going to happen on the day of the event: who will be speaking, who will deal with questions from the floor, etc.

Press kits

- Compile press kits for the event that include all pertinent information about the launch, together with any appropriate photographs

- Make sure a press kit is sent as soon as possible to any relevant media who are not able to attend the event

- Ensure your telephone number is included in the press kit so that you can be contacted after the event for additional information.

Special media requirements

- If radio and television representatives are expected, discuss in advance of the event the facilities they require and the timing of the interviews

- Try to 'pre-sell' exclusive story angles to a variety of publications and media in advance of the launch.

USEFUL TIPS

- *Whatever you are launching – a new magazine, car, restaurant – the same basic rules apply.*

- *Decide on a theme for the launch which could involve a particular venue, colour, dish, costume.*

- *The media are interested in a story – so create an interesting, newsworthy angle for them.*

- *When deciding on a date ensure that the chief executive and key media can attend.*

- *Don't go overbudget with the venue and make sure that it is convenient for the majority of guests.*

- *Send invitations out, if possible, three weeks in advance, to all the relevant media. Telephone all invitees on the day prior to the event.*

- *Book a photographer to take colour and black and white photographs, which can be offered, to the media.*

- *Brief the client prior to the event.*

- *Compile an interesting and comprehensive press kit for non-attendees as well as attendees.*
- *Try to 'pre-sell' exclusive story angles to select media prior to the launch.*

12 Crisis public relations: How to handle emergencies

The guidelines

The major part of this chapter has been written by Doug Goodman, Managing Director of Doug Goodman Public Relations and former head of PR for Britain's largest holiday company. He writes on how you should prepare and cope with an emergency, shows how good planning pays dividends and offers some useful case studies. But first we consider some general principles.

Not all that a public relations officer touches results in favourable coverage. If only that could be the case! So, what should be done about unfavourable coverage or in the event of an emergency?

PR practitioners naturally endeavour to ensure that every piece of coverage is favourable. But though they may succeed in getting the media to visit a particular restaurant, a TV crew into a particular hotel, the city editor to meet a particular chief executive, or a specific editor to visit a particular factory, there is no guarantee that coverage will result from the exercise, or that, if it does, it will be favourable. A good PRO will do everything to ensure that all the arrangements go smoothly, that everyone is briefed, and that the 'positive', favourable facts and angles are presented. But at the end of the day – and this is the big difference between advertising and PR – even with the most professional PR assistance, one is ultimately in the hands of the media.

Generally speaking, if unfavourable coverage does result, the best advice is to forget about it, and move on to the next exercise, unless, that is, the piece of coverage is by a majority vote positively unfair and damaging, when an approach to the editor/news editor is in order or, in the final analysis, to one's lawyers. Making a fuss at other times is unlikely to achieve anything except frayed tempers.

When there *has* been an emergency, such as a fire, death or any other major disaster within your organisation, it is advisable to follow a set rule of procedures in order to try to ensure that the incident is portrayed accurately and fairly to the media.

Any of the above events could result in headline news in your area and possibly even nationally, so it is important to realise that special steps should be taken to ensure that the company or organisation's point of view is represented and that any questions are handled with the organisation's best interests in mind. If the PRO is not on duty then the most senior person should assume the following responsibilities:

- Before attempting to make statements to the media, the PRO designate must instruct all staff and personnel that no one other than the appointed spokesperson or team is to communicate with or answer questions from the media or public. All enquiries should be channelled through the spokesperson in order that replies are consistent

- Take the names, addresses, telephone numbers and fax numbers of the media who have contacted you. Also note the time they rang and any deadlines they have to meet

- Make sure home telephone numbers of individual, management representatives are kept on file in order that you can communicate with them out of office hours

- The PRO designate must take control and should tell the media that a representative of the organisation will phone back as soon as possible; he or she must never appear to be negative and should always assume an authoritative attitude

- Develop a statement that clarifies the organisation's position. Discuss this with the police if they are involved; invariably they will also be preparing a press statement at the same time

- If death, injury or accident have occurred, you should never release names or addresses of those involved without first checking with the police to ensure that the next-of-kin have been informed. And it's usually wise to let the authorities make the notification as they are trained in the required skills

- Read your statement to the press and avoid being drawn into further discussions unless you are clear what your reply will be

- In most circumstances, an initial statement such as 'we are investigating the incident' will suffice until a more detailed response has been researched and prepared.

Crisis PR in practice

Doug Goodman, Managing Director of Doug Goodman Public Relations:

Stop and think about the worst possible situation that could occur in your organisation. As an in-house PR executive or a consultant, what sort of crisis or problems are you likely to be called on to handle?

Think back over the recent past to the tragedies which have hit the headlines all too frequently and perhaps offer a silent word of sympathy to the PR practitioners and other members of organisations who have had to resolve many varied problems and maintain the good name of their company.

PR can only be one of many tools employed in the problem-solving business: a good management team, adequate communications, security and administration groups and staff or customer welfare teams must all play a role. And most fundamental of all must be a company policy of caring about people, of putting welfare and safety before profit. A company which has sloppy procedure or an attitude of not caring about the customer will inevitably be exposed.

All too often company management decides to call in the PRO as the disaster unfolds and expects the PR expert to take the pain away. Just as you cannot learn to give a good TV interview as you head towards the studio, public relations cannot solve a problem when it is brought in too late.

The right place for PR is at the top, reporting to the managing director or a very senior person. The PR executive must guide and advise, must know about everything happening in the company or in the client's organisation and, most important of all, he or she must anticipate.

A key role for PR is to work closely with senior company staff to devise and implement a plan for handling disasters. Any company not prepared for a small problem or a major disaster is inviting trouble.

What do we mean by a disaster? Try to recall some of the headline-hitting stories of recent years. Some will have occurred where no possible blame can be attached to the organisation, others will have been caused by rules being broken or poor working practices.

In Britain in recent years there have been air, rail and sea disasters – notably the Townsend Thoresen ferry tragedy and the Thames pleasure boat sinking, oil rig incidents, sabotage of supermarket products including the Perrier problem and many others. What all these have in common is that customers' safety and welfare were at stake and that the image of the organisations would suffer if the correct action was not taken. It is all too easy to decide in retrospect what the action should have been and how the outcome might have been different.

But if a company comes out of a disaster with its reputation destroyed, its customer confidence lost and its staff morale in shreds, then quite clearly something went wrong! So can PR prevent things 'going wrong'? Yes, in certain circumstances it certainly can and should be involved in the planning of appropriate procedures and courses of action for dealing with disasters. PR should also be involved in the training of key people and the rehearsal of scenarios; in the counselling and advising during an incident; in damage limitation or turning potentially bad news into the positive; and in evaluation and discussion after the event.

While a large company may have further to fall than a small one if it mishandles a problem, the small one needs to be just as adequately prepared. Big organisations can devote the resources to disaster management more readily than the smaller companies so there may be a need to investigate the use of specialist PR consultancies that can be called on to advise and help.

Taking disaster management seriously: An example

One large organisation which takes disaster management very seriously is Thomson Tour Operations, the UK's biggest tour operator. With so many clients spread around the world it is inevitable that when incidents like terrorist activities, health problems, strikes, natural disasters occur, they will become involved.

It is a philosophy based on care of the client and quality of service which ensures that Thomson has the resources and experience to deal with problems. While some organisations believe it could never happen to them, at Thomson the belief is 'not if, but when'.

Highly experienced specialist teams are available in the company with resources which expand to match any need. At the company's head office in London a permanently staffed operations centre with a very sophisticated information and communications network is at the heart of the system. Key people who can assemble special teams at very short notice are on permanent call and precisely defined procedures ensure that everyone knows his/her role.

While PR would have a very high profile during the handling of an incident it is successful teamwork which stands out.

The leisure business in general is very newsworthy and holidays in particular provide a vast amount of material for the media. Most of the time the press coverage is good but when problems occur on holiday the press is quick to report the events. It is a sad fact of life that one Briton mugged in Spain will gain more column centimetres than a natural disaster affecting thousands of people in the Far East.

The media is generally very fair and I can recall very few occasions during my time as head of PR when the media failed to request and publish a company spokesperson's comments at the end of a critical item. It is vital therefore that adequately trained staff can always be contacted by the press.

It is the PRO's specific responsibility to ensure that staff are available every minute of the day and night, are fully briefed on current events, are aware of company policy and an agreed statement and are trained to deal with anything from a peak-time television news interview downward. The release of information to the press must be strictly controlled as only a few key people are permitted to make a comment.

Much emphasis is placed on short- and long-term preparation and practice. Regular radio and TV familiarisation courses are held in order to give management the opportunity to go through the very worst situations which could be encountered.

The up-sides and down-sides of every problem are written down and analysed, while role-playing helps define the key points which the company spokesman must make.

Rehearsal is of tremendous value. This was proved when BBC Radio 4 wanted an early morning comment from the company on how the latest Basque bombing campaign in Spain was likely to affect tourism. The very same questions had been rehearsed the previous evening.

As part of its disaster management plan, Thomson holds exercises where various groups participate, at very short notice, in major incidents. Strengths and weakness can be pinpointed and procedures improved. On one occasion 50 people took part in a simulated coach crash. The PR department played a prominent role as, unknown to them and the directors, a press conference had to be arranged at ten minutes' notice for national press, radio and TV who arrived at the company's head office.

The head of PR had been 'written out' of the day's exercise and was able to muster an army of extras as well as a professional film unit to take the parts of very demanding press people. The final version of the film, which was edited and presented like a TV news item, showed up a number of deficiencies. For example, the 'press' had not been prevented from interviewing 'bereaved' clients; insufficient control of the press conference was apparent; company spokespeople gave conflicting statements.

As a result of the rehearsals and regular group discussions, methods of disaster management are being constantly refined and updated.

SECTION TWELVE

A major concern in the PR group is always whether sufficient numbers of them would be available at the time of an incident. With foreign travel taking up a large part of the members' time, some of the executives could be absent at any given moment.

The first two hours after an incident are crucial in press-relations terms. During that time the PR team must assemble, establish policy, prepare and issue a statement and an emergency phone number, brief the company spokesperson and prepare for several hundred telephone and face-to-face interviews.

Previous experience has shown how vital it is to take the initiative and act, rather than react, during these first few hours.

It is unlikely that a disaster will unfold at a convenient 10.30 am on a Tuesday and be resolved by the end of the day. It will happen at the worst possible time. To overcome the concern at having insufficient PR resources, a back-up team of 12 could be summoned to run a press information centre.

The press's needs tend to unfold in a predictable way: the Press Association and the national papers, radio and TV get the news within 20 minutes, the provincials call within two hours and the weekly papers make contact two days later asking if anyone from their area was involved.

Good and extensive contacts within the media are of such fundamental importance to the PR practitioner that the point needs no stressing. Tip-offs and advance warning from the press about incidents can assist the PRO greatly.

In one incident, a senior journalist phoned to advise the PRO that reports had just been received of an aircraft crash in the Canary Islands. No other details were available but the journalist would call back exactly two minutes later to check whether it was an aircraft chartered by Thomson. That professional kindness enabled the PR head and operations team to check that all company flights were safe and to establish that, tragically, one operator's aircraft was indeed missing. When the return call came two minutes later, closely followed by dozens of others, adequate resources were in place to give accurate information immediately.

In an average week the press and PR team at Thomson Tour Operations will handle several hundred press enquiries. The vast majority of these written and telephoned requests are of a routine nature but several will concern holiday problems. Most problems arise through an event which is entirely beyond the control of the company. An illness, accident or death has occurred and the press wants to know what action has been taken. Strikes or terrorist activity may disrupt holiday arrangements and again the press requires information on how the company is handling the situation and looking after the welfare of its clients.

On the rare occasion when the press follows up a story where a client has complained about accommodation being below standard, building work or service of a low quality, the company may well be at fault. Not only must accurate information be given to the press but the situation must be fully investigated to ensure that, if necessary, things are put right.

But what both types of problem have in common is that they require prompt, accurate and honest answers: prompt because newspapers have deadlines and if information is needed in 20 minutes then after lunch will not be acceptable; accurate and honest because if you lie you will be caught out and no one will ever trust you again.

Being accurate and honest does not mean always divulging everything. When a client books a holiday with Thomson, a confidential contract is made so such details as names and addresses will not be released to anybody – except when the police request it. This rule naturally applies to press requests for client information and, however demanding these requests become, the rule is not broken. This is a very sensitive area and must be handled with care.

On many occasions a problem which might have resulted in adverse press coverage has been turned to the company's advantage. Holiday-makers hospitalised overseas or repatriation by air ambulance have provided good human-angled stories which had a happy ending through the care and concern shown by company staff.

'John praises holiday reps', says one headline. 'Their staff were wonderful and did everything to help us', a couple were reported as saying after a robbery.

'Thanks to prompt action by Thomson staff our daughter got the best medical treatment possible', another paper said after an accident in Greece.

Nothing spectacular, you might think. Staff were only doing their job. Nevertheless it is gratifying to see a potentially critical story turned to one which demonstrates genuine care for the customer.

The value of good communications was demonstrated when a terrorist bomb destroyed a parked aircraft in Sri Lanka. The Thomson representative advised the company operations department who in turn called the press officers at home to tell them that the four passengers on the programme were safe and wished to continue their holiday.

When the press called for a comment the company spokesperson was able to respond at once with the details. So efficient are the overseas staff and operations personnel that the press offices are often called late at night with information about what might seem fairly trivial accidents or incidents. But it is better to have too much information than none whatsoever.

To ensure that a company spokesperson is always available the press office is staffed from 8.00 am to 7.00 pm, and during evenings and at weekends radio pagers and mobile phones are used.

For example, the world's worst nuclear disaster – the Chernobyl power station explosion – tested Thomson to the full. The company operates a year-round programme of holidays to the USSR and at the end of April 1986 it had 274 clients in

Moscow and Leningrad. From the time the news arrived in the West until their clients were brought home, staff experienced the five most intensive days for many years.

Teamwork was the key to the success of the operation and while a fairly small number of people were directly involved, many more contributed. A video film was made by the company some weeks after the event and the teamwork was reconstructed to show others in the company exactly how disaster management plans had worked.

Although there were no Thomson clients in Kiev, the nearest tourist city to Chernobyl, Moscow was only 400 miles distant. As the size of the disaster became known and reports suggested that radioactive clouds were drifting eastwards, Thomson sought assurances from the USSR and from British nuclear specialists. Nobody was prepared to state that no risk existed so under company policy, which puts health and safety before all other considerations, guests and staff would have to be brought home.

The first phone call to the company's office in Moscow drew comments about the weather. News of the seriousness of the situation had not yet reached them. Letters were prepared for the clients in Moscow and Leningrad advising them of the situation and plans were made to send an aircraft to bring them home.

By this time the Western press was carrying headlines like 'thousands dead' and 'nuke hole of death' and interest was focusing on Britons 'stranded in the USSR'.

A statement was issued to the effect that all tours to the USSR had been suspended by Thomson and the news was carried by BBC TV. The press office worked at full stretch issuing bulletins and answering questions. The operations department investigated the many and varied methods of 'rescue'. The client welfare department handled large numbers of calls from worried relatives and friends of those on holiday in the USSR.

The continental department took the key role of maintaining communications with Moscow. This involved keeping a phone line open for several days and using it without a break. The phone bill came to over £4,000.

To arrange a special flight over Soviet territory takes weeks under normal conditions. Every hour was critical. The Foreign Office in London was asked for help and diplomatic staff in Moscow tried to speed up formalities. The first day of May arrived and on May Day the Soviet Union closes for national celebrations. The aircraft, which had been standing by, was required elsewhere. The first day of the company's summer programme began, putting more pressure on the operations department.

A growing volume of press questions were asking what the tour operator was doing to bring its passengers home. Just after midday on 1 May official permission was granted.

A further complication had arisen before departure on the ten-hour roundtrip. Radiation-detection equipment set up at Heathrow to screen arriving passengers was not to be made available. Detection equipment had to be put on the aircraft and letters of advice on health checks written and distributed to passengers.

The home landing was scheduled for 6.00 am at Gatwick and the focus of the press turned to the arrival of the first package tourists from Russia. The company had to consider whether its clients would wish to be greeted by the media. The Thomson press team announced that senior staff and representatives, who had been working in the USSR, would be available at a press conference at the airport.

As the first returning clients, accompanied by Thomson staff in full uniform, came through the barrier, cameras closed in and the press began their interviews. Comments were positive and the company was praised for its action and concern shown by staff.

At 8.00 am on 'Breakfast TV News', the report from Gatwick ended with Doug Goodman saying that his company's first priority was always the safety and comfort of its holiday-makers. A carefully prepared plan and professional approach had ensured that a potentially damaging situation was turned to the company's advantage.

Conclusion

By now the importance of the right philosophy must be apparent and adopting the attitude of 'it can't happen to us' is inviting disaster.

The key points for the PR executive or the consultant called in by a client are these:

- Anticipation
- Preparation
- Action.

USEFUL TIPS

- *All possible incidents and disasters must be anticipated and their effect on the company analysed.*

- *Preparation must include the written production of a disaster manual, the selection and training of staff to deal with different aspects of the event, particularly media handling.*

- *A rehearsal of the groups of people involved in any disaster plan must be held.*

- *When disaster does strike, the carefully prepared procedures will ensure that the event is handled with a professional and caring attitude.*

Hawksmere Publishing

Hawksmere publishes a wide range of books, reports, special briefings, psychometric tests and videos. Listed below is a selection of key titles.

Masters in Management

Mastering business planning and strategy *Paul Elkin*	£19.99
Mastering financial management *Stephen Brookson*	£19.99
Mastering leadership *Michael Williams*	£19.99
Mastering negotiations *Eric Evans*	£19.99
Mastering people management *Mark Thomas*	£19.99
Mastering project management *Cathy Lake*	£19.99
Mastering Personal and Interpersonal Skills *Peter Haddon*	£16.99
Mastering Marketing *Ian Ruskin-Brown*	£19.99

Other titles

The John Adair handbook of management and leadership – *edited by Neil Thomas*	£19.95
The inside track to successful management *Dr Gerald Kushel*	£16.95
The pension trustee's handbook (2nd edition) *Robin Ellison*	£25

Sales management and organisation
Peter Green — £9.99

Time management and personal development
John Adair and Melanie Allen — £9.99

Everything you need for an NVQ in
management – *Julie Lewthwaite* — £19.99

The management tool kit
Sultan Kermally — £10.99

Working smarter
Graham Roberts-Phelps — £15.99

Desktop Guides

The company director's desktop guide
David Martin — £15.99

The company secretary's desktop guide
Roger Mason — £15.99

The credit controller's desktop guide
Roger Mason — £15.99

The finance and accountancy desktop guide
Ralph Tiffin — £15.99

Reports and Special Briefings

Dynamic budgetary control
David Allen — £95

Evaluating and monitoring strategies
David Allen — £95

Software licence agreements
Robert Bond — £125

Negotiation tactics for software and
hi-tech agreements
Robert Bond — £165

Achieving business excellence, quality and
performance improvement
Colin Chapman and Dennis Hopper — £95

Compliance with CDM regulations
Stuart Macdougald-Denton — £125

Employment law aspects of mergers
and acquisitions – *Michael Ryley* — £125

Mergers and acquisitions – confronting
the organisation and people issues
Mark Thomas — £125

An employer's guide to the management of
complaints of sex and race discrimination
Christopher Walter — £125

Securing business funding from
Europe and the UK
Peter Wilding — £125

Influencing the European Union
Peter Wilding — £125

Standard conditions of commercial contract
Peter Wilding — £139

To order any title, or to request more information, please call Hawksmere Customer Services on 0207 824 8257 or fax on 0207 730 4293.